Aganetha Dyck
The Power of the Small

On the Series

The Canadian Artist Monograph Series (CAMS) consists of books that focus on presenting the work of Canadian artists. Each volume in this series explores the practice of a single artist, actively participating in the arts and culture of Canada, through critical texts, interviews and copious images.

Series Editors
Miriam Jordan-Haladyn & Julian Jason Haladyn

Aganetha Dyck
The Power of the Small

JULIAN JASON HALADYN
with MIRIAM JORDAN-HALADYN

CAMS
Blue Medium Press, 2017

Copyright © 2017 Julian Jason Haladyn
"A Note on Other-than-Human Beings" Copyright © 2017 Miriam Jordan-Haladyn
"Aganetha Dyck and William Eakin's *Light*" Copyright © 2017 Miriam Jordan-Haladyn and Julian Jason Haladyn
Image copyright © by Aganetha Dyck
All rights reserved

Edited by Miriam Jordan-Haladyn
Copy editing by Madeline Lennon and Émilie Uzoma Jacob
Images courtesy of Aganetha Dyck [except where indicated]
Design by Julian Jason Haladyn

Cover image:
Hive Scan [detail], 2001-2003
collaboration between Aganetha and Richard Dyck

First Edition

ISBN: 978-1-988101-02-6
Published by Blue Medium Press
London, Ontario, Canada
www.bluempress.ca

Contents

Acknowledgments	vii
A Note on Other-Than-Human Beings by Miriam Jordan-Haladyn	1
The Power of the Small by Julian Jason Haladyn	**3**
Early Works: Political Economy of the Household	10
Honeybees, Habitus and Consciousness	36
Moments of Interspecies Communication	68
Aganetha Dyck and William Eakin's *Light* by Miriam Jordan-Haladyn and Julian Jason Haladyn	**111**
Conversation with Aganetha Dyck by Julian Jason Haladyn	**123**
1. The Bees	125
2. Dialogues	140
3. Small and Large	151
4. New Works	168
List of Figures	187
Bibliography	199

For Peter

Acknowledgments

Peter and my family have been extremely important during my long career as an artist. My first wish is to thank Peter Dyck. He was my assistant throughout the 20 years of working with the honeybees. He created specific beehives to suit every bee related project, packed completed bee works, constructed shipping crates and documented my work; he also had his camera at the ready while we were at the hives. While there, he often started the smoker and held it at the ready if the honeybees were worried. He calmed the honeybees. Peter has been at my side throughout my career and I give him much credit for my being able to work freely with the honeybees.

   I would like to thank my family for their assistance, especially for their research into international honeybee news. Michael, Diane, Patricia, Richard and Deborah have been supportive throughout my career. I thank Richard for the apiary sound recording and his collaboration during the production of the Hive Scans. Deborah has been my invaluable office assistant for many years, taking care of correspondence such as answering queries, sending documentation and images upon request. Michael, Diane and Patricia have never stopped their generous and ongoing assistance and encouragement.

   There are numerous scientists and beekeepers who have generously shared their bee related knowledge and research. I would like to thank Dr. Mark Winston for his first visit to my studio, which resulted in my spending a week in his bee lab at SFU where I was given free rein to study honeybees with him, his assistant Heather Higo and several graduate students. Dr. Stephen Pernal and Andony Melathopoulos in Beaverlodge Bee Lab, in northern Alberta, offered much information on their indoor and outdoor lab. Most importantly, I was invited to observe the artificial insemination of a Queen Bee by Dr. Maria Spivak, distinguished Entomologist from the University of Minnesota who was visiting the lab. And Dr. Otis at the bee lab in Guelph Ontario gave me much information on honeybees and allowed me to visit his lab housing global honeybees of many colours and sizes. Henry and Rita Funk continually helped me by sharing their use of found materials within their apiaries. And thanks to Phil Veldhuis for his assistance with the bees for about the last 20 years, during which Phil generously gave his time and knowledge of beekeeping to me. His guidance is part of the reason for my successful career working with the bees.

    I thank the artist William Eakin for many years of photography and apiary assistance towards our two person exhibition *Light*. To Wanda Koop for friendship and being there when times get tough. To my extraordinary studio mates Reva Stone and Diana Thorneycroft for over 23 years of sharing studio space downtown. To Megan Krause, part time studio assistant. I thank Carol Phillips for her generous support over the years. She was the very first curator to give me an exhibition. Thanks to Dr. Stephen Borys and staff at the Winnipeg Art Gallery, Meeka Walsh and Robert Enright at Border Crossings Magazine, as well as Director Gilles Hebert and staff at The St. Norbert Arts and Cultural Centre. I also want to express my appreciation to The Canada Council for the Arts, The Manitoba Arts Council, The Winnipeg Arts Council and MAWA Winnipeg for supporting my work. Finally, thanks to Julian and Miriam for their patience, interest and writing that made this book a reality.

—Aganetha Dyck

From the moment I proposed this project Aganetha has been nothing but supportive, sharing with me documentation of her practice, including the work she produced during the time I was writing. I thank her for all the time and effort she spent helping me, for the amazing work she creates and the wonderful stories she shared. This book is truly a collaboration that I undertook with her – and we both dedicate it to her partner Peter.

While researching and writing this book I have had the support and encouragement of numerous people. I thank Jamelie Hassan for introducing Miriam and I to Aganetha, as well as Janice Gurney, Andy Patton, Madeline Lennon, Ron Benner, Mireya Folch-Serra and Maxwell Hyett for the many conversation on Aganetha's work. For sharing her interest in bees, I thank my sister Kimberly who corresponded with Aganetha, sending her napkins she had made with bees embroidered on them – which, Aganetha told me, reminded her of her grandmother's embroidered handkerchiefs. I thank Elizabeth Legge for her support and for sharing with me her stories of getting to know Aganetha, including her purchase of *Merry Christmas Mr. Kooper*. For their help preparing and editing the final manuscript I thank Madeline Lennon and Émilie (Lili) Jacob.

Most of all I want to express my gratitude to Miriam Jordan-Haladyn for her help throughout this project, as well as for allowing me to include our collaborative text "Aganetha Dyck and William Eakin's *Light*" – an early version of which was published in *Fuse* magazine. Miriam helped with every aspect of this book, including the idea of other-than-human beings, which is invaluable to my approach.

—J. J. Haladyn

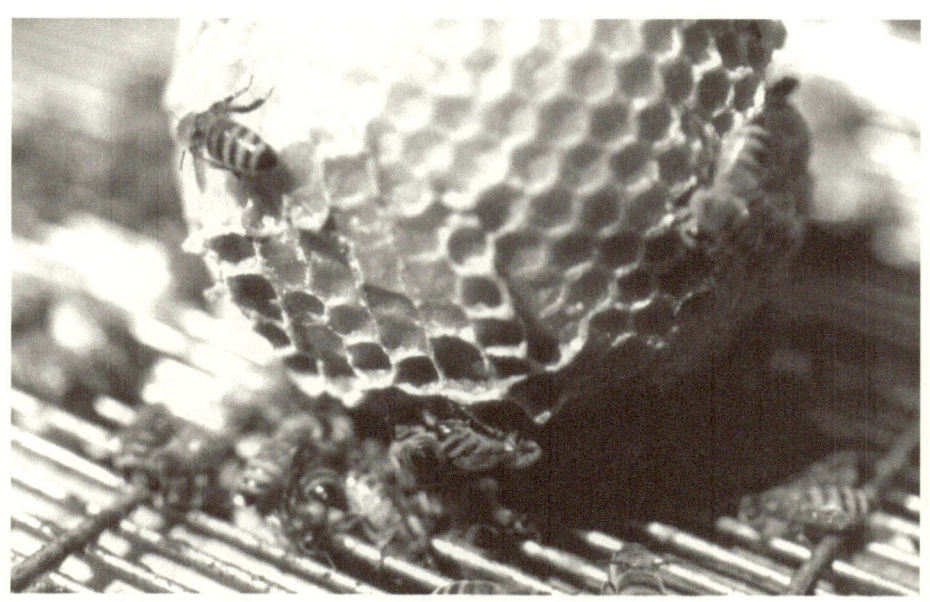

0. Honeybees working on *Sports Night in Canada* [baseball], 1995
   installation view at St. Norbert Arts and Cultural Centre Apiary
   images courtesy of Aganetha Dyck

A Note on Other-Than-Human Beings
by Miriam Jordan-Haladyn

In Iroquoian thought the land is a living being. This is not simply metaphor, but an actual fact. We call the land *Yethi'nihstenha Onhwentsya* which means "she-to-us-mother provides-(for us)-needs." All living beings gain sustenance and material form from *Yethi'nihstenha Onhwentsya* quite literally our very bodies are made from the materials of the earth and we survive and grow strong from the fruits that the earth provides. This is a non-Western conception of being, in which humans and other-than-human beings are part of a balanced world view. The world is literally alive, from the tiniest rock, to plants, animals and humans. We all need each other to survive.

      An other-than-human being is another living being that is necessary for life. An other-than-human being is simply another being that has a different form and way of living in the world.

The Power of the Small
by Julian Jason Haladyn

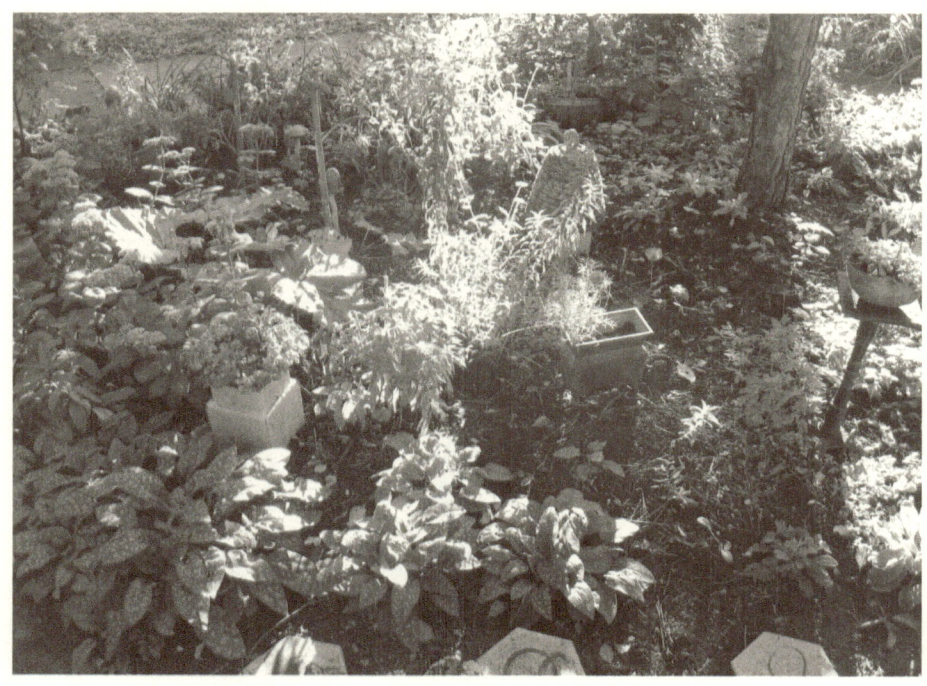

1. Aganetha and Peter Dyck's Garden at their house on Dunrobin Avenue in Winnipeg, 2010
   photograph by Miriam Jordan-Haladyn

September 2010, I visited Aganetha Dyck's studio in Winnipeg with Miriam Jordan-Haladyn and Jamelie Hassan. While Hassan had known Dyck for years, Miriam and I had just met her the night before, soon after arriving in the city.[1] Yet Dyck drove the three of us around Winnipeg all day and even had us over to her house for dinner that evening with her partner Peter – there was a beautiful garden out front.

That afternoon she brought us to see her studio, located in an older building in the downtown core; casually we walked around the space as she showed us various projects, old and new, some of which she had to unwrap (plastic to protect the beeswax) and several came with fascinating stories. Having seen a number of her beeswax-covered sculptures in museums, which are typically presented as isolated or contained displays, experiencing the dialogue of materials and information within this studio environment provided a unique perspective into her practice. We viewed her artworks surrounded by stacks of apiary boxes, research (books, photographs, drawings), supplies for making her work (blocks of wax, a two-burner hotplate) and documentation – including a photograph of the artist and Her Excellency the Right Honourable Michaëlle Jean[2] from when Dyck received the Governor General's Award for Visual and Media Arts in 2007. After an extended visit and intense conversations we moved on, but not before Dyck gave us catalogues and several photographs related to her work.

This current study emerges directly out of my experience in Dyck's studio, extending the ideas that developed from seeing her work as a form of exchange enacted through the physical and conceptual qualities of her practice. From her early shrunken sweaters and canned buttons to her long-term work with bees she has consistently engaged in what could be characterized as different forms of material dialogues, much of which is based within the reciprocal relations of humans with nature (meant in the most general sense) – or, to use Miriam's exceptional phrase, between human beings and *other-than-human beings*.

This is not a grand project for Dyck, nor is it an attempt at proposing an ideal of nature as source or ultimate truth. Rather her work suggests a modest and often-understated sense of the ways natural elements and beings can be seen as offering different material-based perspectives on the world, such as the manner in which wool shrinks when heated or the fact that bees will build patterns of honeycombs on any object. In a sense, she demonstrates an alternative to the manner in which human language is (arbitrarily) imposed onto the natural world – a tree being a *tree* only because the word 'tree' is assigned to describe it – by allowing nature, as a type of language, to affect existing objects and our understanding of their relations. Dyck plays with the powerfully creative properties of the natural world in her practice, treating them as at once serious and humorous, personal and social; and it is these same properties that form the basis for the dialogues enacted through her work.

The most important relationship for Dyck is with bees, an ongoing exchange that has come to inform her

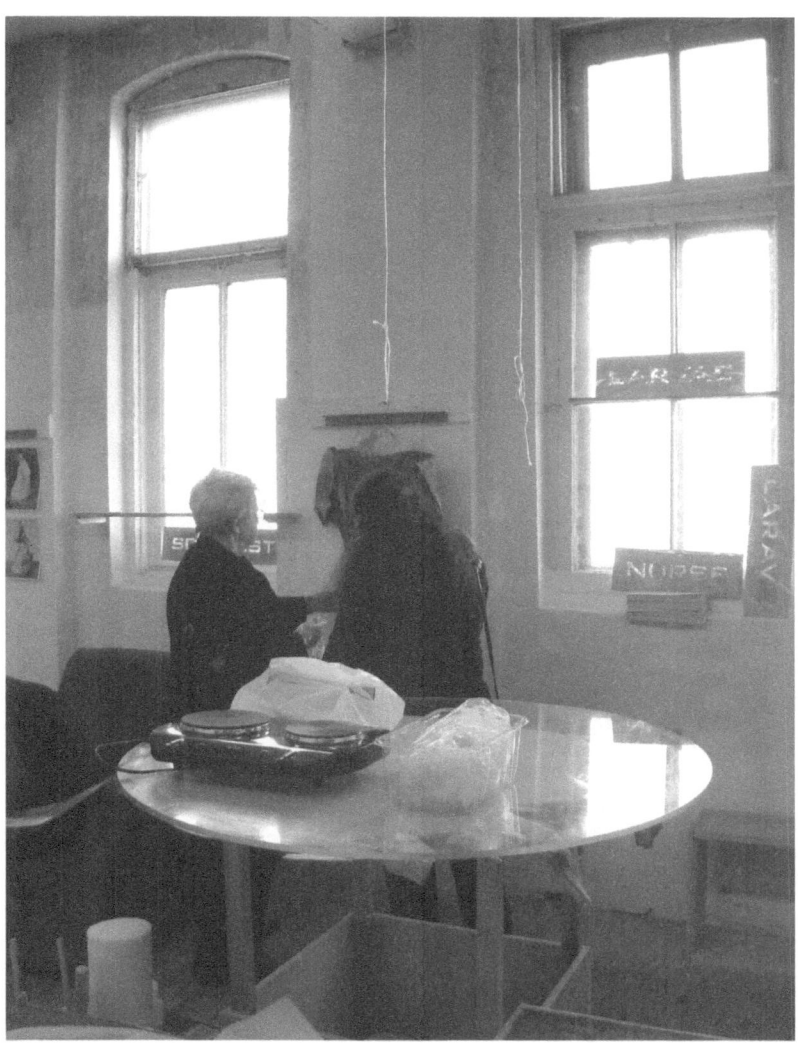

2. Aganetha and Jamelie Hassan in Dyck's studio, 2010

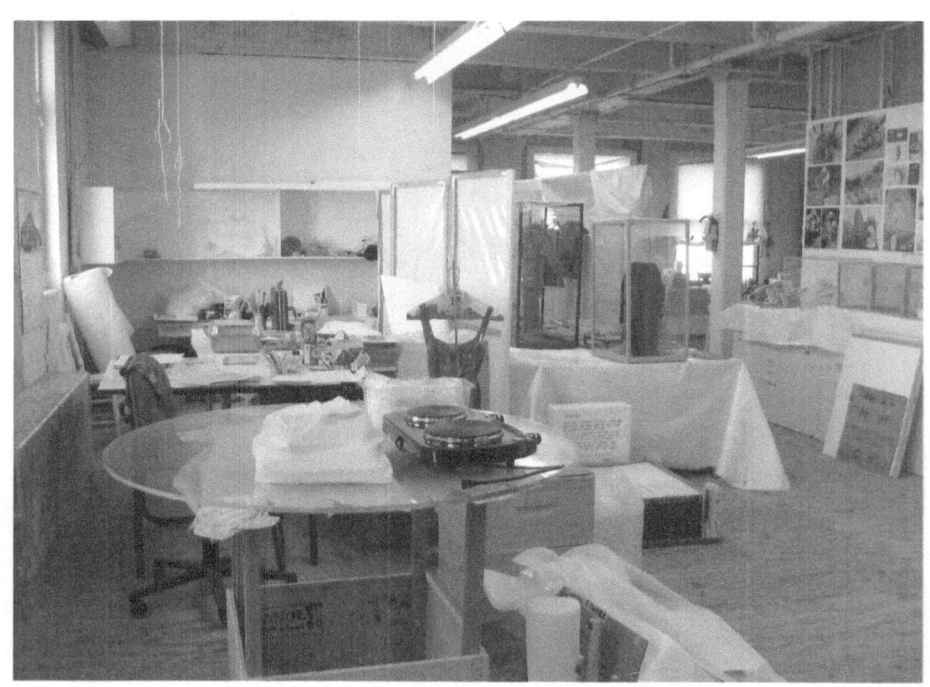

3. View of Dyck's studio, 2010

entire artistic outlook for over twenty-years. This is the aspect of her work for which she is best known. Her name is virtually synonymous with images of honeycomb-covered objects, ranging from sports equipment and miniature figurines to Braille poetry and signs of words related to the bees. We examined several of the metal signs placed in the windows of Dyck's studio, including *Pupae* (2007-2008), *Nurse* (2007-2008) and two versions of *Larvae* (2007-2008). While Dyck's overall relationship with the bees is discussed in detail later in this text, here we should recognize the extent of her engagements with these little creatures, who do not simply alter readymade objects for the artist but rather actively collaborate with her, and she with them, in order to create the works. By allowing the bees to alter words that we use to reference them, as well as the people related to them (such as "beekeeper," "scientist" and "artist"), Dyck quite literally gives the bees a chance to respond to us in their own way. The possibilities of language and communication, especially as enacted through material forms of exchange, are defined in relation to "the power of something so small," as she describes the bees to Sigrid Dahle.[3]

Dyck has also referred to this last concept as *the power of the small*, a beautiful phrase that has been adapted as the title of this book. In my understanding this idea is not limited to her bee works but instead is an integral part of her entire artistic practice. The concept of the small is used as a framework for discussing and analysing Dyck's major projects to date, which includes her early works with sweaters, buttons and cigarettes as well as, and most prominently, her work with the bees.

Early Works: Political Economy of the Household

For Aganetha Dyck, the creative act is not limited to the realm of art but also and necessarily must include life, understood in a broad sense. We are not talking here about life in the abstract, as an ideal or some other conceptual category, but rather the everyday lived modes of creativity that she engaged in as a homemaker before – as the story of her career goes – starting to make artworks at the age of 38. "Born late in the Depression and raised on a Manitoba grain farm near Marquette by her immigrant Mennonite parents, Dyck's sense of beauty is intimately connected to a sense of the well-worn, the used, the second-hand, to objects that make up the fabric of daily existence," Shirley Madill points out, a perspective that forms the basis for the artist's "application of domestic processes to fine art production."[4] In Dyck's practice the desire to reconcile life and art – one of the major tenets of a progressive vision of art within modernity – is an extension of the creative possibilities inherent in mundane experiences and activities that are often overlooked, such as those performed in the private sphere of the home.

While the artist herself claims that her "artistic career began in 1975," when she started taking art classes with George Glenn at Prince Albert Community College, I want to suggest that her creative practice begins much earlier and is part of her everyday work as "a housewife and a mother."⁵ Rather than a departure, what we see in Dyck's earliest artworks is a continuation of many of the activities, objects and processes she engaged in as a homemaker of the 1960s and 1970s: washing and drying clothes, working with buttons, canning, Polaroid photography and cigarettes.

*

One of Dyck's earliest projects involved the intentional shrinking of woollen clothes by repeatedly washing the garments until they had shrunk as much as the properties of their materials allowed them. Most people have experienced this process accidentally, while washing and drying clothing, finding that a sweater or pants or dress are no longer the proper size but have instead become miniaturized – retaining their basic form but now only fit for an homunculus. Purchasing an old washing machine for her studio, Dyck adapts this unwanted domestic occurrence as a way of creating a large series of sculptural objects, produced from 1976 to 1981, collectively known under the title *Sizes 8 – 46*.

In the creation of these works she literally continues performing a task that she had been engaged in for much of her life, except now Dyck was self-consciously adapting the process. "I was using homemaking techniques like washing and then ironing and all kinds of things I was doing in the house," she tells Roger Balboni and Sylvie Marandon. "It was like discovering a new language, an artistic language in doing such things in a studio situation."⁶ This language that Dyck discovered, which she uses throughout her artistic career, is based upon a deep sense of respect for materials and processes. She recognizes the beauty of everyday objects as moments

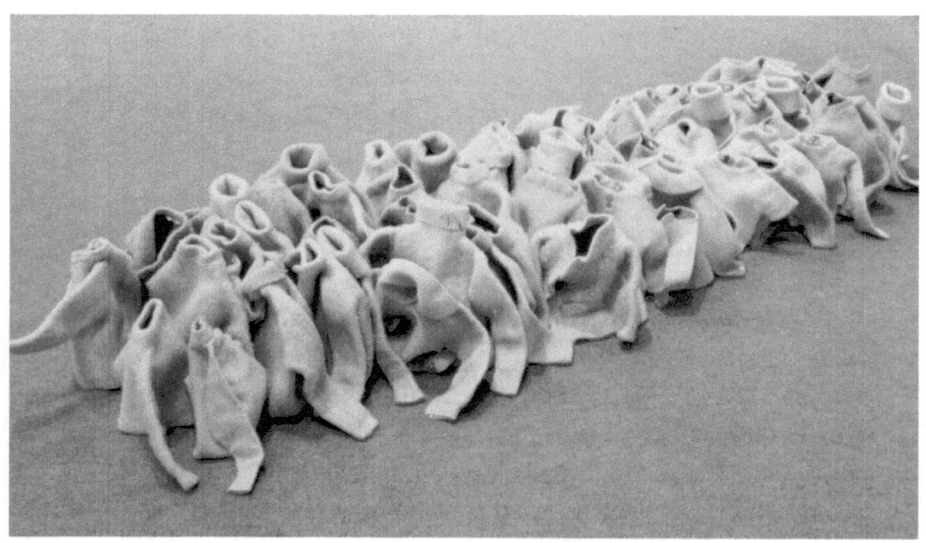

4. *Close Knit*, 1976-1981
photograph by Peter Dyck

of potential insight or knowledge that challenge us to rethink the world, not through logic but rather a conscious consideration of the random or chance encounters that make up our lives. Rather than irritation, what if we allow ourselves to see past the self-interested problems that result from accidentally shrinking a piece of clothing and instead consider the (natural) ways this process transforms found materials into unique works? What if we allow this 'mistake' to occur and enjoy the marvel of the readymade objects created?

Within the large body of shrunken garments that make up *Sizes 8 – 46*, which the artist estimates at over 600 items, there are a number of smaller groupings that have been treated or shown independently by Dyck. I want to call attention to several that I consider to be the most significant and show a diversity of approaches within this overall series.

In *Close Knit* (1976-1981), we see a column or procession of 65 shrunken sweaters clustered together, presented as one work. All the garments have a similar lightened colouration – white and off-white with subtle tints of yellow and beige – that serves to visually unite them into a singular form, which looks like a minimalist rectangle made out of little pieces of altered readymade clothing. If this work shows the coming together of these miniature items, *Shrunken Clothing On the Road* (1976-1981) pictures the escape of a series of such sweaters, which appear to be journeying joyously down a dirt road. These photographs are less singular works than the documentation of an imaginary event that Dyck stages with her miniature garments, this time sporting a variety of colours. As they appear "to hobble up a country byway," Nancy Tousley suggests these works "take the saying that 'clothes make the man' and wring it out of shape."[7] In

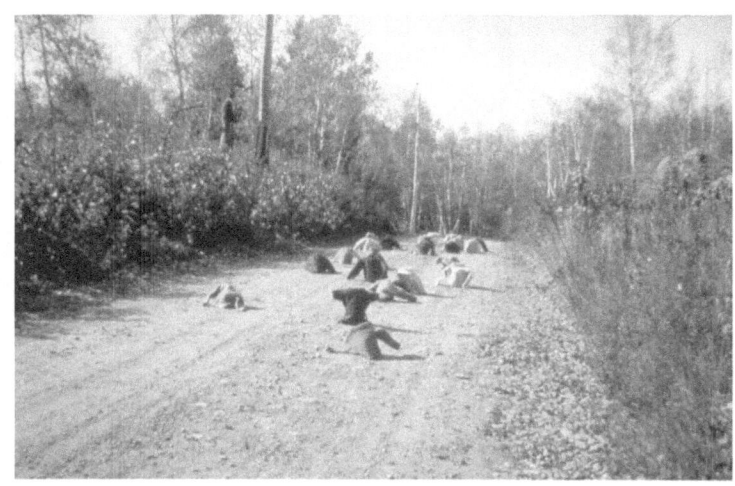

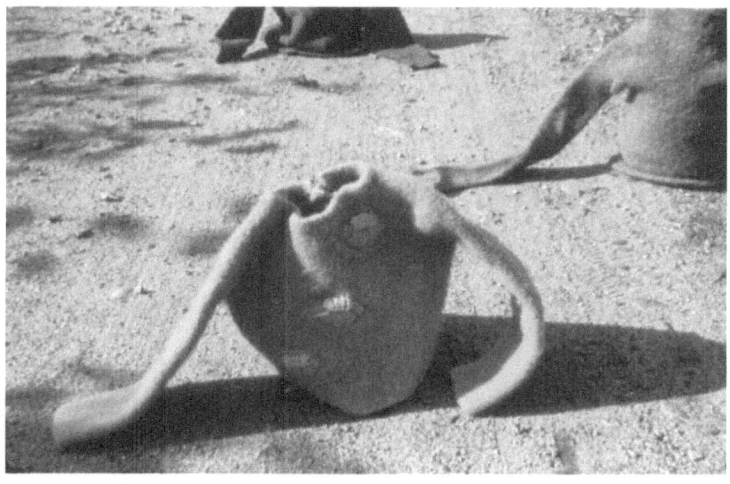

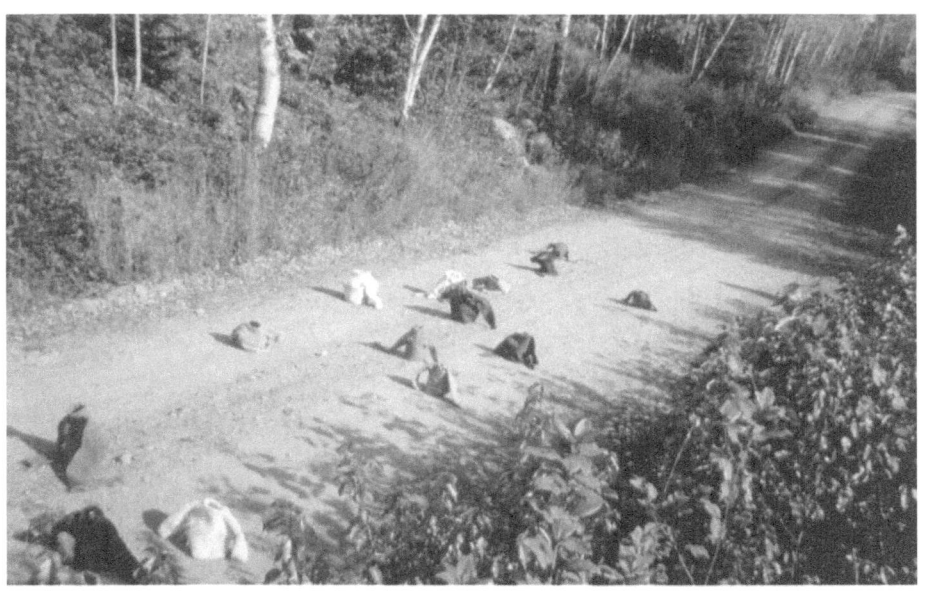

5-7. *Shrunken Clothing on a Road*, 1976-1981
   photographs by Peter Dyck

this reading the shrunken clothes are primarily interpreted anthropomorphically, as playing with or critiquing their relation to the human body – an approach not uncommon among the various treatments of works in this series.

Yet, I want to suggest another interpretation that instead focuses on the way Dyck, very much in the tradition of Marcel Duchamp's readymade mode of artistic production, presents already existing objects from everyday life as works of art, a shift in perception that we, the spectator, are asked to accept. While these items may retain the sense of a previous symbolic relationship to the human body – in the same way the urinal of Duchamp's *Fountain* (1916) cannot elude associations with bodily functions – the point is that this connection has been intentionally abstracted, making our previously self-interested response no longer valid.

Dyck highlights this abstract or conceptual quality in her more elaborate works, such as *Merry Christmas Mr. Kooper* (1981). Here we are presented with a shrunken sweater accompanied by a series of dominoes, which are all the same. The title is both playful and personal, making a literal reference to the act of gift giving that made the work possible, since the dominoes were given to her by Wanda Koop, whose father Mr. Koop wanted Dyck to have them. By giving Dyck this 'useless gift', Mr. Koop and Wanda Koop collaborate in discovering a 'use' for the dominoes through active and creative shifts in multiple people's perceptions of this (originally disappointing) everyday object.

I also have a personal connection to this work, which is part of the private collection of my friend and colleague Elizabeth Legge. Here I am using her photograph of the project, as installed in her home (the dominos are asymmetrical in this installation because of the constraints

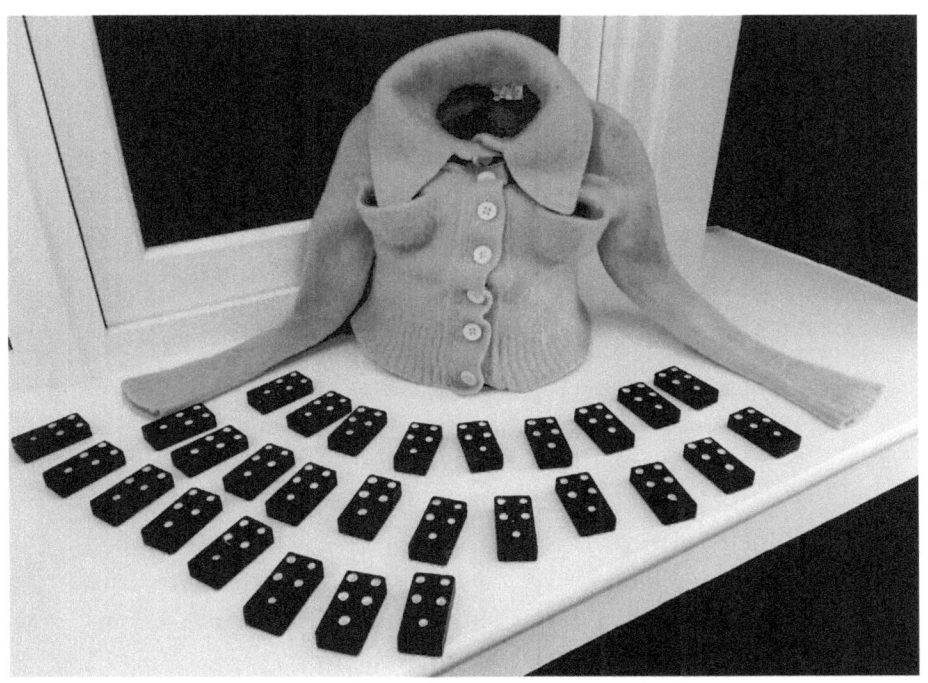

8. *Merry Christmas Mr. Kooper*, 1981
   photograph by Elizabeth Legge

of the window ledge). When I asked what interested her in the work Legge wrote:

> I was drawn to the humour (all the dominoes identical, like a practical joke had been played on Mr. Kooper – who gave Aganetha the box when he got them, as he knew it was the kind of thing she'd love), and by the great classical Venus-like restraint of the pocket/breasts! That is, it's beautiful and funny. A jest of fate or sabotage in the domino factory (Duchampian!) meets up with incompetent "housewife's" work meets up with minimal seriality.[8]

What we encounter when viewing the miniature form of these shrunken garments has less to do with their previous existence – as clothing meant to cover a human body – and more to do with how we choose to personally experience them in their creative potential, beyond the givenness of their function. This is Dyck's gift: she is able to offer us a vision of the world as both the same and different, normal and special, communicable and incommunicable, serious and fun – subverting our expectations.

The playfulness of Dyck's vision of art is readily apparent in *Shrunken Clothing On the Road*; it is hard not to laugh at the sight of the wondrous adventure of these little artworks into the world. Or to enjoy the humour of the mischievously titled *Merry Christmas Mr. Kooper*, an artistic "practical joke" that we participate in by interpreting its qualities and thus making it part of our lives. Dyck – again like Duchamp – sees the necessity of including play in the practice of art. In fact, it is the discoveries of play that account for the way her career as an artist emerges out of the familiar domestic practices she engages in, out of watching a sweater get smaller and smaller with each wash. "I remember when I shrunk my first clothes," she told Sigrid Dahle, "I just laughed and laughed because they were so tiny."⁹

For me, Dyck's shrunken clothing culminates in the works of her series *Hockey Night in Canada* (1981). Comprised of numerous woollen winter toques that have each been shrunk to the size of little cups, these colourful objects appear to have an active sense of play that, especially within the context of Canada, likely invokes nostalgic memories of watching hockey and even, for some of us, playing while trying to stay warm. Taken from the well-know television program Hockey Night in Canada, which airs NHL games, the project's title draws us into personal and cultural memories of a shared community brought together through a mutual enjoyment of the game.

I have fond childhood memories of sitting with my father, grandfather and mother as we all cheered – and screamed – at the television, rooting for one team or another; and it is impossible to separate these moments from the excitement I felt when playing hockey, either at the local rink or, more often, with friends on the road out front of my house (I was the one with the hockey net!). One can almost hear the well-worn phrase: *put on your hat, it's cold outside*.

Such feelings of nostalgia are accentuated by the miniature stature of these hats, which are far too small to be worn anymore. Shown together, this series of shrunken toques present an overview of the familiar patterns of such headwear, with important adornments such as the hanging tassel or whimsical pom-pom – calling attention to the power of objects to mark time and space, especially in lived experience. While my interpretation of *Hockey Night in Canada* is at times

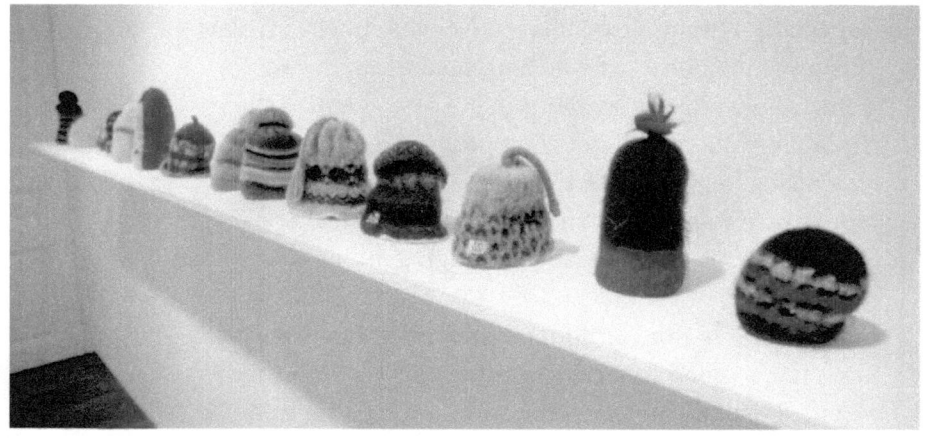

9-11. *Hockey Night in Canada*, 1981
photographs by Peter Dyck

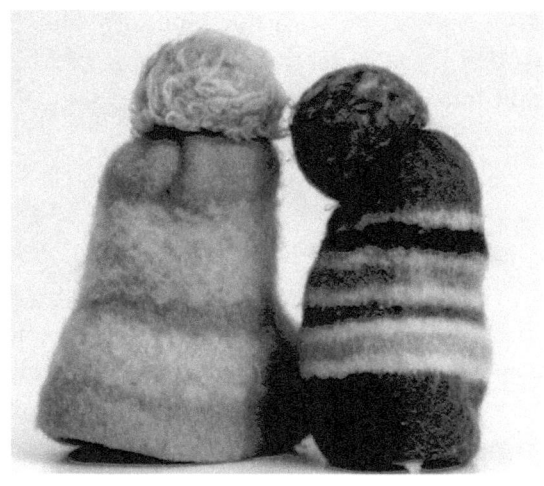

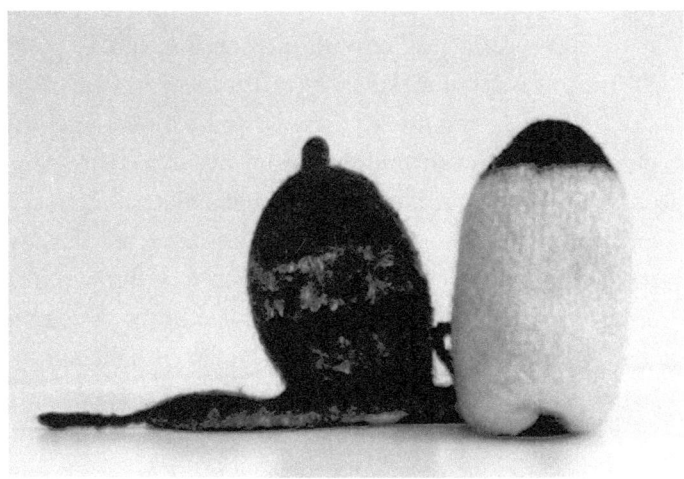

overtly personal, it is just this kind of reading into the object that Dyck's practice encourages, in which art is brought into contact with life.

*

A key characteristic of Dyck's working method, of her approach to art generally, is a desire to explore in depth specific relationships and process, both situational and durational, with the objects she examines. In the case of her *Sizes 8 – 46* series this meant repeatedly shrinking garment after garment, performing the same act of intentionally washing (in hot water) and drying over 600 articles of clothing until they could not shrink anymore. The two additional early projects I want to talk about involve a similar logic, with the canning of over 600 jars of buttons – from a "stash of millions of buttons," as she told me – and the altering of some 1,000 cigarettes; Dyck's devotion of the remainder of her artistic career to an intensive examination of the bees also qualifies. Such excessive attention to single procedures goes far beyond the experimental need to know what will happen or the simple joy of watching the items of clothing get smaller.

Instead, this is a creative form of habitual behaviour grounded in her perception and appreciation of the object-oriented processes she engaged in while maintaining her house and family (working with clothes, a washing machine, refrigerator, Polaroid film, suit cases, buttons, glass bottles and the like). Such actions and perspectives represent a fundamental system or scheme, a *habitus* the nature of which is explored throughout her practice as an artist.

Habitus – a Latin term that originally referred both to a person's disposition and dress or attire[10] – is an adaptive concept that describes the "system of internalized schemes that have the capacity to generate all the thoughts, perceptions, and actions characteristic of a culture."[11] Pierre Bourdieu builds upon Erwin Panofsky's use of this scholastic concept to develop a means of addressing the ways people in particular cultural or social contexts share, most often unknowingly, fundamental systems of behaviours and dispositions that regulate most of the specific views and perspectives they develop. As a theory of practice, *habitus* defines an individual's ability to enact and embody cultural schemes, which function not as strict rules to be followed but rather as general parameters that can be adapted to a variety of situations throughout life; a consideration of *habitus* allows us to analyze the ways in which individuals are practitioners of the culture they inhabit, which forms a type of vocabulary for the production of subjectivity and subjective meanings.

For Aganetha Dyck, a woman living in the Canadian prairies in the 1970s, her interest in working with the vocabulary of her *habitus* – including practices such as maintaining her home, raising and caring for her children and husband, being an active member of her community, among others – necessarily relates to the fundamental systems that guided a great number of middle-class Canadian women of her generation. These are shared cultural activities that, while made individual by the uniqueness of each person's experiences, reflect a larger sense of the behaviours and meanings inherent in this particular time and place; the creative potential of these schemes is based within the idea of "discovering community at the very heart of individuality in the form of culture."[12] Dyck's use of *habitus* in developing a practice of art is manifest in the adaptation and expansion of domestic activities, objects and processes, practical systems that she creatively and self-consciously deploys in her role as an artist.

*

In her discussion with Sigrid Dahle, and elsewhere, Dyck makes it clear that she does not see her practice as a response to 'women's work', but rather as a way of exploring the creative possibilities that emerge when the treatment of such *work* – and its related objects – is not limited to questions of the practical.[13] She does not use a washing machine to critique the limitations of her life as a homemaker (who is required to endlessly perform the boring task of washing clothes), but rather to demonstrate the excess potential that she sees in the machine's capacities by using it as a tool in her art. While part of our daily environment, we use such devices repeatedly for one single purpose alone, without question. Dyck critically engages with her *habitus* by challenging the prescribed nature of everyday lived existence – of the political economy of the household – which in her hands is allowed to become more than mere practice. Her shrunken garments demonstrate that the act of washing can produce creative and interesting results beyond the practical need to clean clothing.

Similarly, in her series *Canned Buttons* (1983-1984) Dyck uses the practical processes of "preserving for many years animal and vegetable substances in all their freshness and with all their natural properties" – as the discoverer of our modern canning methods Nicolas Appert described it – applying this technique of preservation to a substance that does not need to be preserved.[14] As a common practice in especially rural Canadian

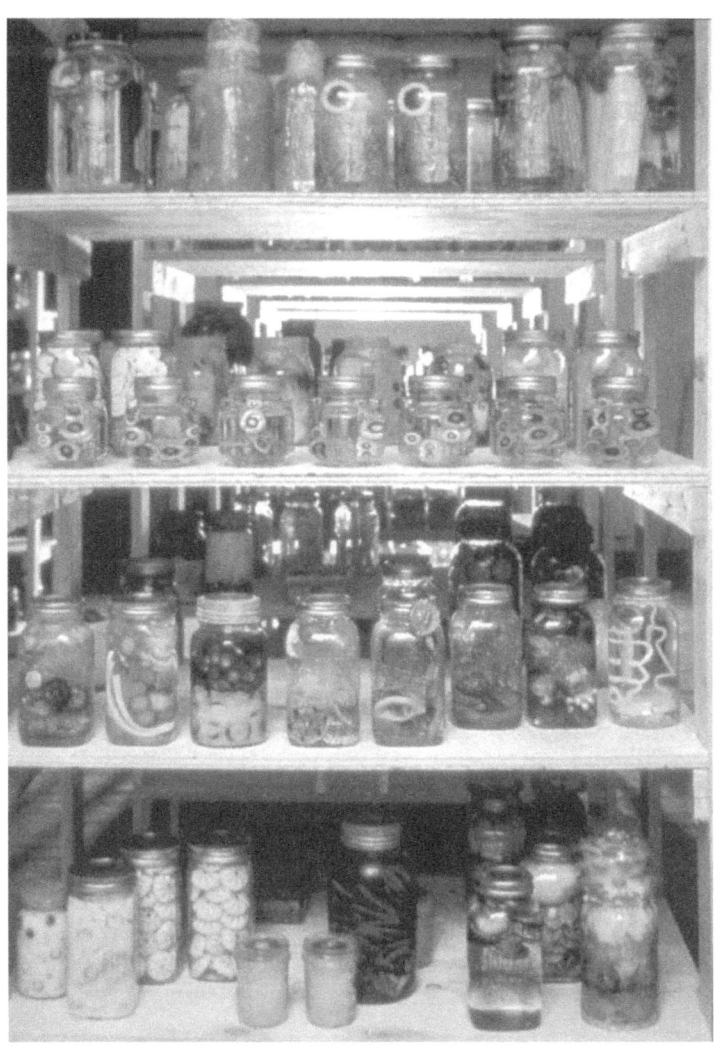

12. *Large Cupboard* [detail], 1984
    installation view at Winnipeg Art Gallery
    image courtesy Winnipeg Art Gallery

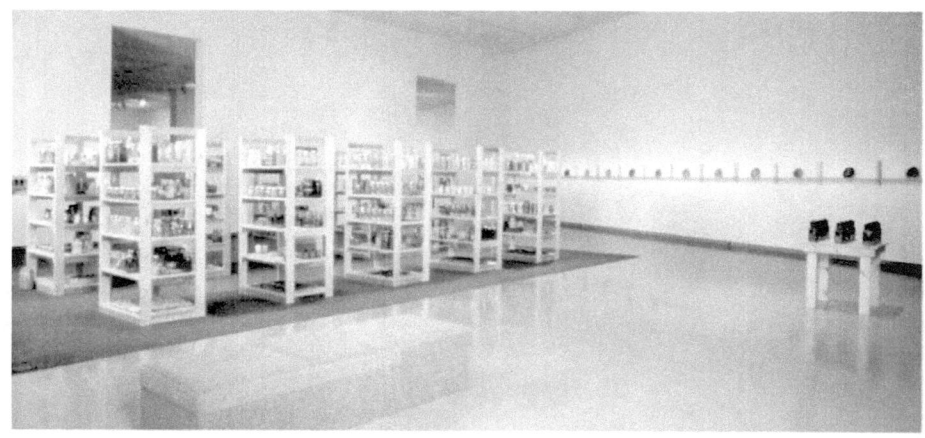

13. *Large Cupboard*, 1984
    installation view at Winnipeg Art Gallery
    image courtesy Winnipeg Art Gallery

communities, canning is deeply connected to issues of family and economy.

Dyck notes that her mother and grandmother engaged in canning; her mother's basement shelves were "filled with colours: tomatoes, pickles, mustard relishes, vegetables, fruit, jams and jellies." In part this is about an economical and, in most cases, healthy way of having food on hand in the home – products that you literally know *what is in them*. But, more than this, canning is also about individuals creating something that they can share with their community, be it immediate family or neighbourhood friends. Unlike mass-produced jam or pickles that one buys at the store, handmade preserves are personal gifts that show connections among the people that exchange them. Dyck's canned buttons adapt not just the techniques but also the larger practice of canning, linking her artworks to this sense of shared practices and meanings.

In her major exhibition of the canned button works, *The Large Cupboard* (1983-1984), we see innumerable glass jars filled with colourful and sometimes abstracted buttons of all different shapes and sizes, displayed on inexpensive wooden shelves – the kind one would find in a basement. Walking into the gallery space it is easy to mistake these for preserved foods, except that, as you get closer, what you see are not tomatoes, pickles, mustard relishes, vegetables, fruit, jams or jellies but instead a wide variety of buttons.

Dyck came into possession of this massive *stash* of little objects when she moved to her 5th floor studio space at 376 Donald Street, which, when she first saw it, was filled with buttons that she excitedly purchased. A few years later, in part inspired by the visual and material qualities of her mother's *amazing* preserves, she began canning these buttons and storing them on wooden shelves in her studio (capturing, in a sense, a portrait of her mother's aesthetic). Her 1984 installation at the Winnipeg Art Gallery reflects the straightforwardness of this arrangement. The main focus of the exhibition is a display of eight readymade shelving units – each with five shelves, including the bottom – presented in two rows of four, forming a multi layered grid into which the jars are located not at random but in groupings based on content. We see, for example, an entire row of smallish jars containing orange-yellow buttons with a dark ring suspended in a clear substance or, to the side of this main display, a separate table that holds nine pairs of (connected) blue jars. Browsing through this collection of processed buttons is a mixture of the familiar and the unusual, moments of recognition that also offer surprises.

In the exhibition brochure for *The Large Cupboard*, Dyck is quoted as saying: "An ordinary button is altered by the use of the canning process. It is placed in a jar, out of context of its intended use. I find this juxtaposition of the absurd and reality a fascinating parallel to life. I am dealing with decay, preservation, death and humour."[15] It is easy to forget that the preservation of food, which now is almost a cultural pastime, was once directly related to survival. Nicolas Appert's invention of canning was the direct result of an award offered by the French government for anyone who could discover a way of preserving food for long periods of time, which was needed for especially military troops on extended voyages at sea. Dyck also talks about the ways early pioneers in Canada and northern United States grew food, which needed to be preserved if they were going to survive the harshness of the winter months. So why does she apply this method, one that is historically tied to issues of life and death, to the canning of buttons?

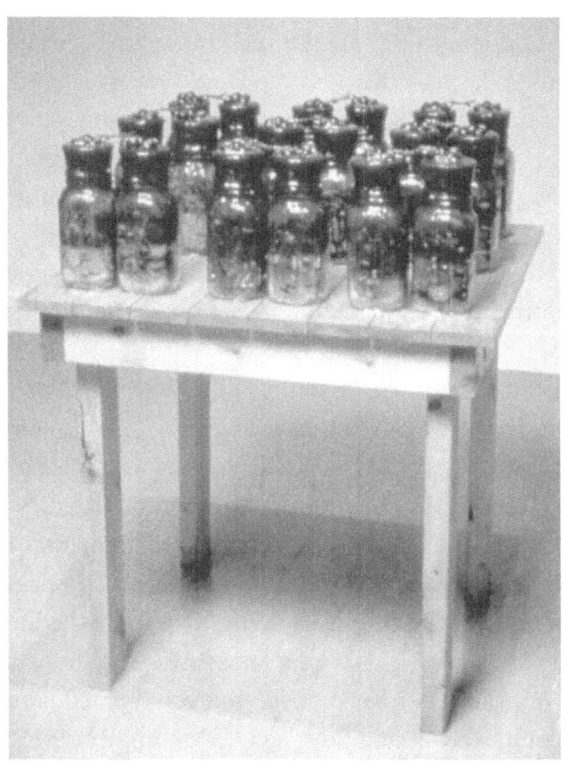

14. *Canning table*, 1984
    installation view at Winnipeg Art Gallery
    image courtesy Winnipeg Art Gallery

There is of course a sense of humour to this act, as the artist rightly acknowledges. It is one thing to store buttons in glass jars – a common home organizational practice – but it is quite another to go to the preposterous and comical length of "preserving" the *natural properties* of buttons through this involved and time-consuming process, particularly in the volume the artist produced.

However, there is another answer to the question of why she canned buttons, one based within the critical juxtaposition between the reality of the practice and the absurdity of the works produced through this practice. Dyck's canned buttons draw attention to the vital importance of creative acts within life, which are responsible for the invention of new ways of preserving food or saving lives and new ways of seeing and experiencing different realities. Instead of just laughing at the image of little buttons floating in their jars, we can also recognize the artist's use of the excess potential inherent in the canning process, which she manifests by pushing the practice beyond its practical limits into new conceptual and visual territory. Her works take seriously the behaviours and meanings of her objects: the way heated woollen sweaters shrink and how people habitually store buttons in jars. Here the creative potentials of art are understood as a necessity of lived existence, a perspective that is dependent upon acknowledging the adaptive nature that both practices – art and life – share, most notably as creative modes of interconnected processes of knowledge.

*

In making her *habitus* the foundation for her early approach to art, Dyck actively engages in subtle and overt critiques of the political economy of the household within, primarily, modern Canadian culture. Working with objects and ideas relevant to many middle-class women and men at the time, and arguably up to the present day, her practice explores and extends the boundaries of the practical systems of behaviours and meanings that determine much of our specific experience in everyday life.

Like the previous two series of works discussed, Dyck's *Altered Cigarettes* (1987-1988) are the result of recognizing and extending personal and community-based habitual behaviour in order to create works that push the limits of our perception of the objects involved. However, unlike the shrinking of sweaters and canning of buttons, her act of decorating cigarettes was motivated by an explicit attempt to stop the habit for herself and others. Smoking was widespread, one could even say ubiquitous part of life in North American communities through much of the 20th century. For many housewives, including Dyck, smoking was part of a daily routine and an important shared practice within the community – I myself remember as a child being around my mother and her friends and neighbours as they talked in smoke-filled kitchens and living rooms, each brandishing a cigarette in their hand. The highly addictive nature of nicotine and its harmful effects on the body turn the act of smoking into a dangerous habit that is exceedingly difficult to stop. For this reason, by "the mid 1980s there was a big anti-smoking, anti-tobacco discussion in the Canadian press," which Dyck tells us she responded to by applying and receiving "funding to alter cigarettes, cigars and pipes into works of art."[16]

The idea to alter cigarettes – and thereby change their prescribed use – came out of an encounter Dyck had with two young artists in Winnipeg, who shared with her their difficulties in quitting smoking. In a gesture both humorous and serious Dyck invited them to hand over

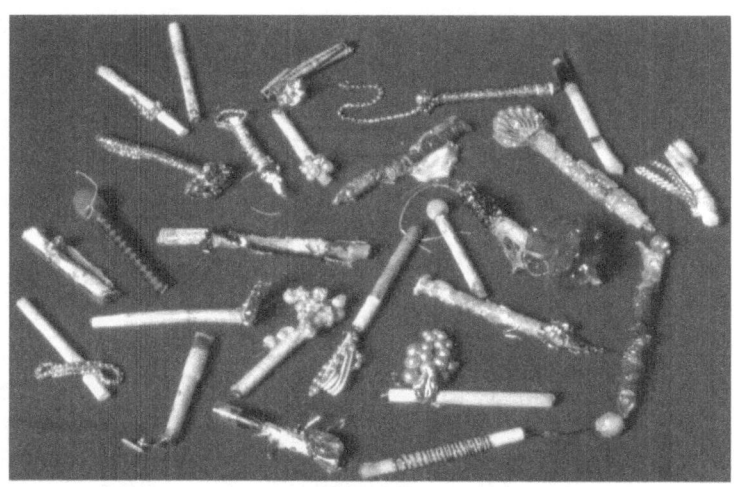

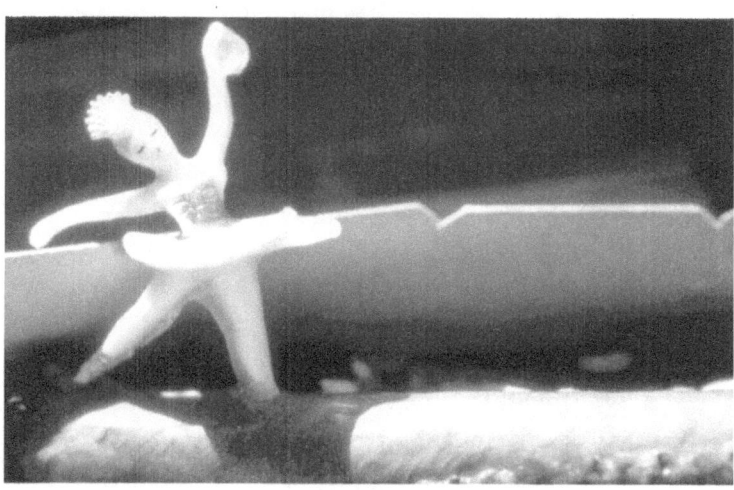

15-16. *Altered Cigarettes and Cigars* [details], 1988
photographs by William Eakin

their cigarettes, which she altered so that it was no longer possible to smoke them, after which she returned the now un-smokable items. Significantly, she literally fetishized the addictive object, rather than throw it away.

Following this event Dyck put out a call to other smokers, inviting them to send her their last cigarette, which she would turn into a work of art with the expectation of an exhibition of the works produced. "I anticipated receiving a hundred smoking devices but received over 1000," she notes.[17]

What started as a personal response within a specific situation became a community oriented project, one based on using her artistic practice as a way of encouraging people to stop their smoking habits. The collection of these altered cigarettes make up the installation *Hand Held: Between Index and Middle Finger*, a witty title that locates the focus of this critique literally in the hands (held between the two fingers responsible for bringing the cigarette up to one's lips) of smokers.

Divorced from their singular function, and through this the addictive and harmful effects associated with their repeated use, these cigarettes took on a new identity as aesthetic objects – as *non-cigarettes*. She dressed them up with all manner of adornments: attaching inexpensive but eye-catching pieces of costume jewellery, small buttons and beads, thread and other everyday items and novelties to these little cylinders most often with paraffin or beeswax. In a particularly striking work, Dyck embeds a miniature plastic ballerina – a cake topper with a tiara and blue tutu – deeply into the textured form of a cigar. This gesture appears less decorative and more violent in nature, punctuating an aggressive quality underlying this series. One gets a

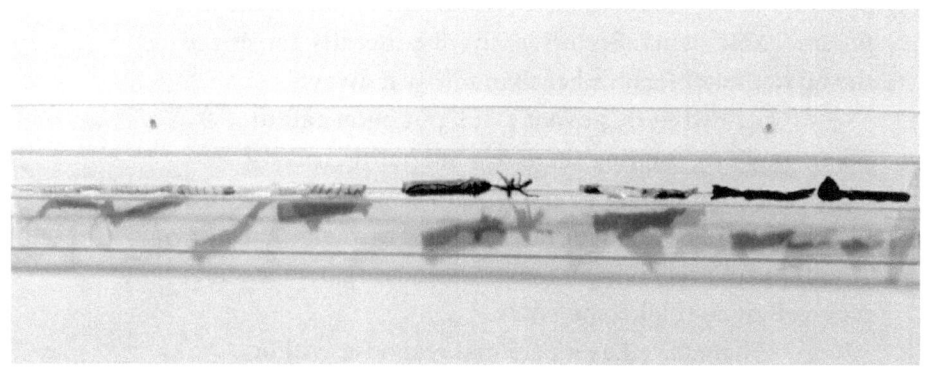

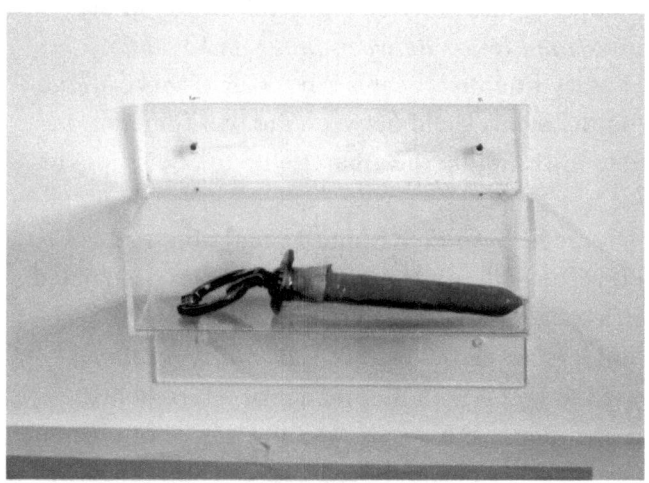

17. *Handheld: Between Index and Middle Finger*, 1988
    photograph by William Eakin

18. *Altered Cigarettes and Cigars*, 1988
    photograph by Miriam Jordan-Haladyn

sense that Dyck's acts of alteration are more serious than they may look at first glance, calling attention not only to the problems of smoking for individuals and communities but also the social systems and structures that support such addictive habits.

It is the conflict between the social and the aesthetic that makes the installation of these altered cigarettes so powerful, which brings the expression of numerous individuals' attempts to stop smoking together into a community of artworks. In *Hand Held: Between Index and Middle Finger* these little sculptures are displayed within a long row of clear, minimalist Plexiglas boxes – each a separate unit – that form a singular line across the surface of the gallery walls, presenting the works as an interconnected series of creative gestures.

During my September 2010 visit to Dyck's studio I was able to examine some of these works up close. In one case, presented alone in a small Plexiglas unit, I saw a wax-coated cigar that had been fashioned at one end with a single dark metal drawer pull – making it look like a surreal baby soother. One aspect of experiencing these works in person, which is lost in documentation, is the strong smell of tobacco that emanates from and surrounds the displays of the altered cigarettes. This is a strong reminder of the material and sensorial qualities that Dyck uses as the base for her intervention, for the creation of these *non-cigarettes* that radically exceed the limits of the practical by denying these objects and the corresponding behaviours a place in the system or scheme that she creates through her artistic practice.

Honeybees, Habitus and Consciousness

During the late 1980s and early 1990s Aganetha Dyck's artistic practice underwent a dramatic change. It is at this time that she began working with the honeybees, creating the artworks for which she is best known. She had started off using paraffin wax to seal the jars in the canned buttons series and to coat and attach elements in the altered cigarettes series, but eventually she switched to beeswax. Because of the quantity she needed, she started purchasing the beeswax from Bee Maid Honey, a beekeeper's supply house. One day Dyck noticed a sign that read 'BEE MAID' made out of honeycomb, which she was told had been created by honeybees; after asking about it she was put into contact with Gary Hooper, the hobby beekeeper whose bees were responsible for the creation of the sign.

      This was the first time she realized the creative abilities of these small creatures, which she immediately recognized as *sculptors*. After this chance encounter – with a honeycomb BEE MAID sign and an amateur beekeeper – Dyck stopped work on her previous projects and started to research the honeybees.

      Why did this experience affect Dyck so profoundly? In part, she seemed drawn to the practical abilities of the bees as naturally creative beings. The sign gave her an initial glimpse at a shared world in which bees and humans work together, creating something that could not have been created by either one alone. The unique qualities of this collaboration between human and other-than-human beings offered her a method for producing works of art through a form of interspecies communication, one that builds upon and expands the conception of *habitus* she developed in her early practice.

If previously her projects explored the creative possibilities that emerge when fundamental systems of activities and behaviours are not limited to questions of the practical, her work with the bees expands the scope of this exploration to include the potential creative acts offered by the behaviours and practices of the honeybees. To rework the statement by Bourdieu quoted earlier: this sign allowed Dyck to discover that at the heart of individuality is a community that extends beyond the human, defined by a more inclusive understanding of culture that for her must include the other beings in the world.

At the core of this shift is Dyck's realization that the vocabulary of practices that she had been exploring may have a parallel in the language of activities, objects and processes used by the honeybees. As such, she seems to consider the possibility that the concept of *habitus* can be adapted to examine the behaviours of other-than-human beings – as seen, almost out of necessity, from a human perspective.[18] In an interview for Mason Journal she states: "Communication and collaboration with the honeybees begins with the acknowledgment and understanding of their ways of existing and their methods of working."[19] The artworks that Dyck creates with the bees are based upon her vision of bridging these two creative practices, the human and the other-than-human, bringing them into a working dialogue that functions through interconnected (interspecies) ways of experiencing and knowing the world.

*

Before discussing the artworks that involve her direct engagement with the honeybees, we first need to consider an intermediary project: Dyck's installation *The Library: Inner/ Outer* (1990-1991). In this series she continues her practice of coating objects with beeswax, like her altered cigarettes, except that in this case it is applied in copious amounts that dominate the forms of the items used – anticipating her iconic honeycomb encrusted works. The result is the creation of books or, more properly, book-objects that bring together adaptive practices of humans and bees. If the book-objects belong to the world of human knowledge, their material treatment, covering them with beeswax, is more properly related to the world of bees and therefore suggests other ways of knowing the world.

In the original exhibition of this project at the Southern Alberta Art Gallery, meaningfully installed in the former Carnegie Library building, Dyck constructs her vision of a *library* as a collection of unique material texts that we are invited to – in an expanded sense of the term – read. Within the space we encounter several key groupings of works that are independent but conceptually interconnected, like sections or chapters in a single book: *Pages, Six Books, Two Books, Pocket Books for the Queen Bee*. A number of these book-objects are presented on their own simple but well constructed black wooden table or, in the case of *Pages* – which appear to be a series of single pages – on their own wooden shelves hung in a row on one wall. All the tables and shelves were made by Richard Dyck with matching proportions and design, visually unifying

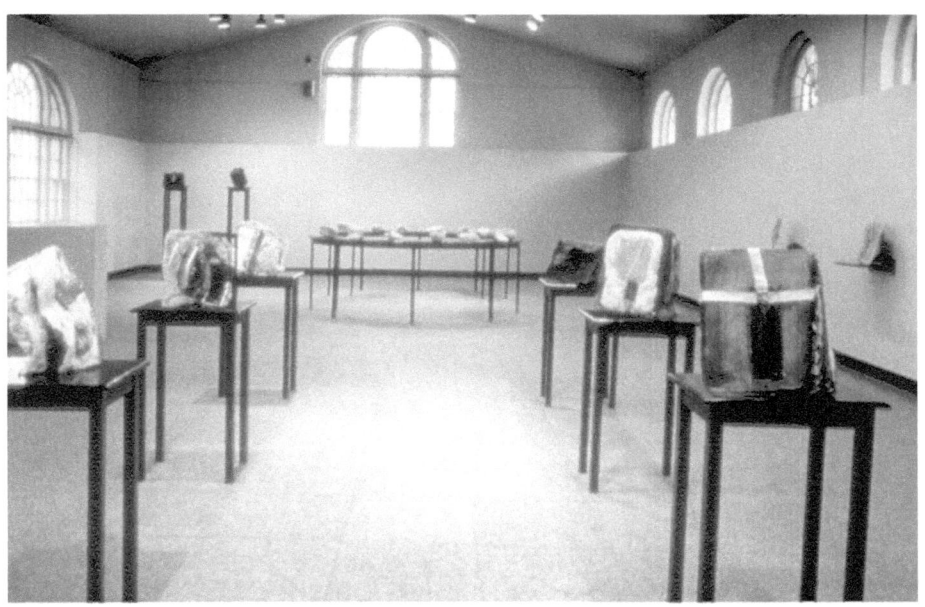

19. *The Library: Inner / Outer*, 1991
    installation view at Southern Alberta Art Gallery
    photograph by William Eakin

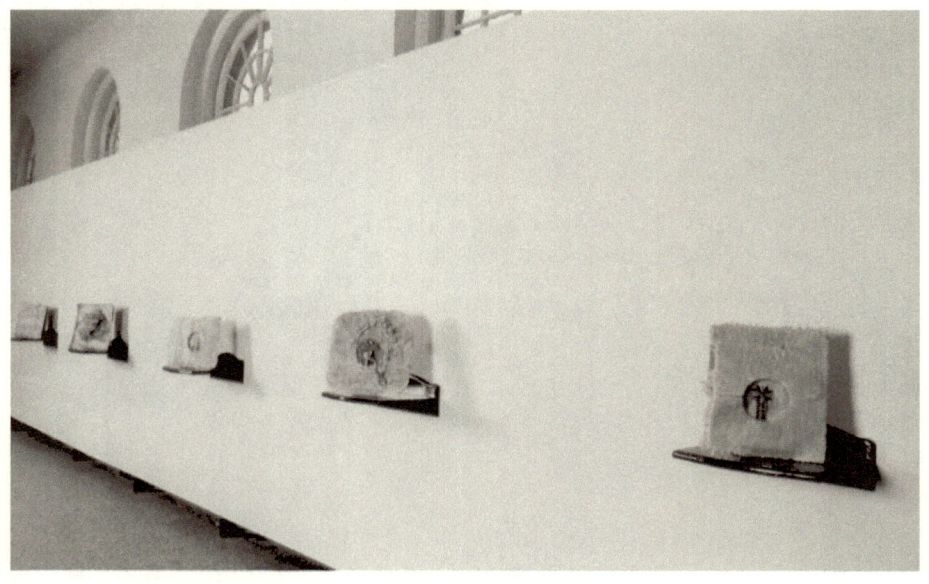

20. *Pages*, 1991
    installation view at Southern Alberta Art Gallery
    photograph by William Eakin

each grouping. For example, in *Two Books* we see a pair of tall tables with little surface space and a small shelf near the floor, whereas in *Six Books* the tables are much shorter, about half the height, with more surface space and no lower shelf. One important exception to this overall mode of display is *Pocket Books for the Queen Bee*, which consists of 16 book-objects arranged on two black wooden tables, each a half-circle that combine to make a full circle with a small space separating the halves. The entire display of the exhibition is unambiguous, even traditional, making it appear like many presentations of books within library galleries.

Yet, the directness of this overall treatment contrasts with the complexities of the constructed book-objects. While it is easy to mistake these beeswax laden works as actual coated books, almost all of them are in reality readymade objects that are presented in place of the book form, both reflecting and challenging this traditional mode of communication. Instead of words, these sculptural assemblages contain a panoply of unconventional signs and material relationships – eyeglasses, glove, artificial flowers, a plastic doll's head, a ceramic statue, Christmas ornament, feathers, a gas mask, plastic necklace, a necktie, drapery hooks, metal door hinge, metal horseshoes, necklace, photographs and newspaper clipping. The logic of the codex is used to transcend the distinction between the page and life.

The materials of lived existence are treated as texts that form a library of corporeal systems of modern human behaviour, which the artist then subjects to the logic of the bees. In other words, the obvious contents of a library (books) are in this case mostly made out of everyday materials (purses, evening bags, briefcases and record album sleeves), which Dyck transforms into book-objects by encasing them in beeswax. This "waxing

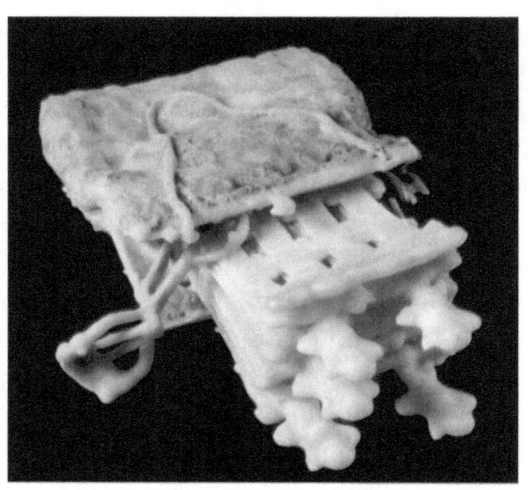

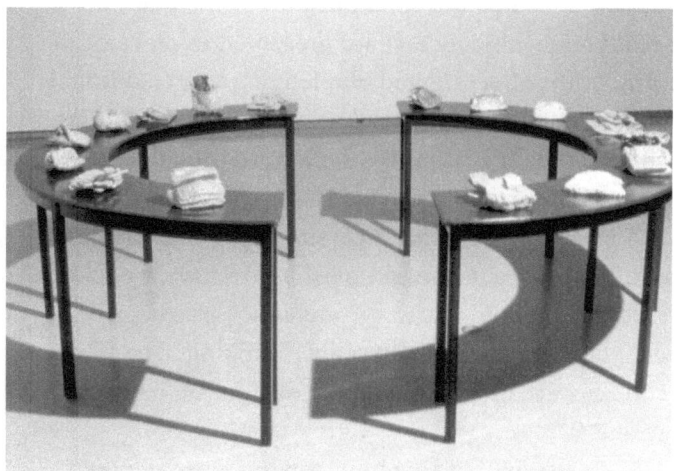

21. *Pocket Book*, 1991
    photograph by William Eakin

22. *Pocket Books for the Queen Bee*, 1991
    installation view at Southern Alberta Art Gallery
    photograph by William Eakin

over," as Joan Borsa notes, "does not eliminate the objects or the meanings they carry, but it certainly destabilizes the original connotations and asks for another reading."[20] The books that Dyck presents in her library all depend upon this language of beeswax, which, through obscuring the original use of the objects and identifying them as 'books', proposes the possibility of experiencing material knowledge and meaning.

In the main display, *Pocket Books for the Queen Bee* (1990), we encounter a group of 16 evening bags and their contents all covered in beeswax. These book-objects are arranged in two groupings of 8 and presented in a circle around two half-circle tables. Understood as pocket books, these works creatively employ the characteristics of this type of printed material: typically small, inexpensive volumes that can easily fit into a pocket, purse or little bag.

There is an obvious parallel being made between the outer forms of the book and the evening bag, which both function to hold particular contents inside (text and/or image in the former, objects in the latter). Yet the layers of beeswax purposefully deny access to any interior space, with even the visible elements we see peeking out of the evening bags becoming exterior, making these book-objects all about the surface of their form – which reflects the way a bee would *read* the object. We are given a narrative here that powerfully invokes the overlapping behaviours of humans and honeybees, while at the same time making it clear that these volumes are specifically meant for the most important being in the bee world: the Queen Bee, whose royal name connects her to a long line of monarchs who for centuries have had books commissioned in their names.

Dyck's library raises questions about the different types of knowledge one encounters, how learning must be understood as something that is not restricted to the page

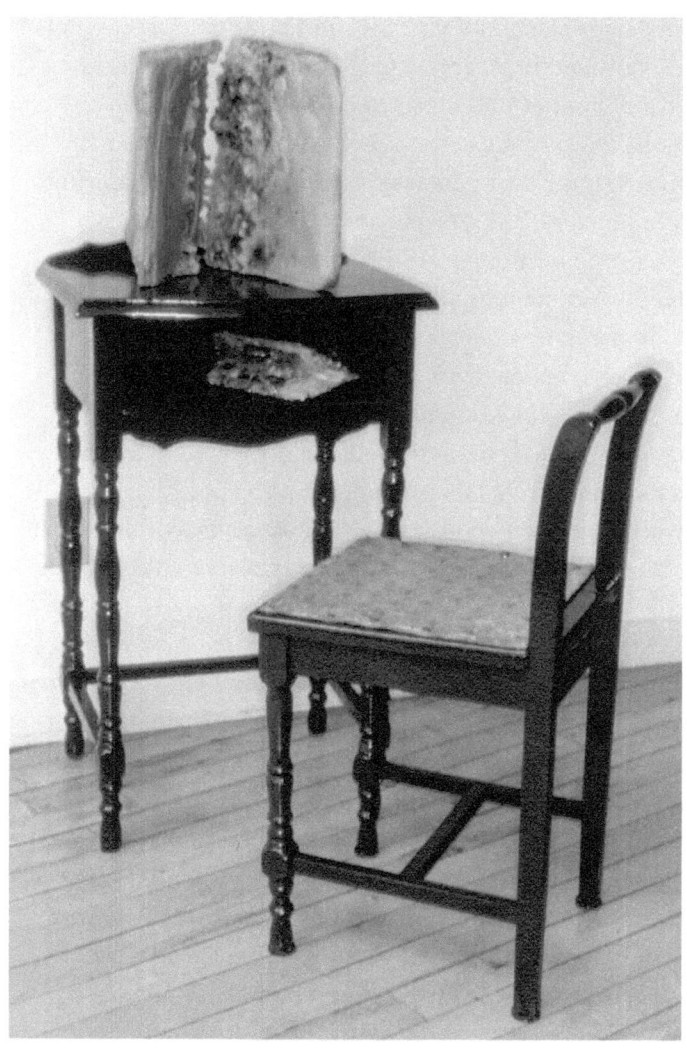

23. *The Queen Bee's Telephone Directory*, 1991
installation view at Southern Alberta Art Gallery
photograph by William Eakin

but instead exists all around us in everyday life, as well as in nature, waiting to be discovered. What can we learn from washing clothes or canning buttons or altering cigarettes? How can the behaviours and practices of bees teach us to look beyond our own human limitations?

In *The Library: Inner/Outer*, Dyck "directly addresses the production of knowledge that is alluded to in all of her previous work."[21] In fact, it is in this installation that she begins to reconceive her approach to art in terms of producing knowledge through a creative dialogue with the behaviours and living processes of the bees. Taken to a bit of an extreme, we might even say that Dyck is attempting to explore what it is like to be a honeybee.

*

The personage that dominates Dyck's library is, without a doubt, the Queen Bee. Not only is she provided with a hive of beeswax-coated pocketbooks, which form the core of the installation, but she is also put in charge of the communications hub of any mid-20th century household: the telephone table. In a work from the periphery of this project, *Queen Bee's Telephone Directory* (1990),[22] Dyck presents a more elaborate display that centres on a telephone book made out of two slabs of beeswax, slightly connected at the bottom, within which are recessed areas that contain honey and yellowjackets.

This directory is mounted on a small readymade black telephone table that has an accompanying chair with an upholstered seat – the type that were once used to hold the telephone, telephone book and/or directory, along with other items related to making phone calls, which were most often located in a hallway (which is why it is interesting that Dyck installed this work outside of the main exhibition space). Unlike the simple designs of the other tables, this set has ornate patterns on the legs and other decorative features that make the work visually distinct. Another interesting difference is the inclusion of a beeswax-covered evening bag tucked away in the space of the shelf, inside of which we see a clump of wax with a stamp on it that reads *Queen Bee*. Here Dyck is equating the practices of the housewife and mother, which keep the domestic sphere of the home running smoothly, with the role of the Queen as the powerful matriarch at the centre of life in the hive.

Let us look briefly at the system that exists in the beehive. Within a honeybee colony there are three types of bees (castes), each with its own particular function: workers, drones and Queens. Most of the tasks necessary to maintain the colony – including taking care of the larvae or brood, building comb and foraging – are performed by the workers; as the only male bees, the drones primary purpose is to mate with a Queen, enabling her to produce fertilized eggs. The central figure in this hierarchy is the Queen, a powerful female bee who dominates the hive. In his book *The Biology of the Honey Bee*, Mark L. Winston describes the Queen Bee in the following manner:

> The aptly named queen reigns over the nest, surrounded by attendants and fed the rich food she requires to perform her few but crucial tasks in the colony. Her slim lines hide the huge ovaries which make her an extraordinary egg-laying machine, capable of laying thousands of eggs a day, and her calm behavior masks her powerful pheromones, chemical signals to recipient workings which control many of their behaviors and provide part of the social glue which holds honey bee life together.[23]

In a very real sense, all of the bees in a hive work for the Queen, with all activities and behaviours being determined, directly or indirectly, by her (often invisible) presence. The Queen's importance is so great that, when a colony loses their Queen, emergency steps are taken to rear a new Queen and, when this is not possible, the result is typically the death of the colony.

When Dyck begins placing objects into the hive it is the worker bees that physically build comb on them, yet this process necessarily engages the entire system of the colony, including the Queen. We must appreciate that the practice of the bees is communal-based and therefore cannot simply be reduced to one part of a fundamental scheme, but instead must be understood as an interconnected system of behaviours and functions. One such behaviour is the manner in which, when an object is introduced into their world, the bees habitually cover it (in part or fully) with wax and honeycomb. Dyck engages with and, in a very real sense, becomes part of this practical system when she self-consciously gives items to the bees, not once but, in many cases, season after season.

It is important to note that this is an extreme moment of trust on the part of the artist, who quite literally gives over control to the bees. If in *The Library* she takes command of the materials, applying beeswax to reflect her vision of the work, in most of her subsequent practice she relinquishes this control and allows the honeybees to sculpt their honeycombs onto the objects through their own processes, as their habits indicate.

In one of the earliest projects that involved her direct engagement with the honeybees, Dyck introduced around 30 pairs of shoes into the hive, allowing the bees to alter them.[24] In addition, she also performed her own alterations that include the application of beeswax–

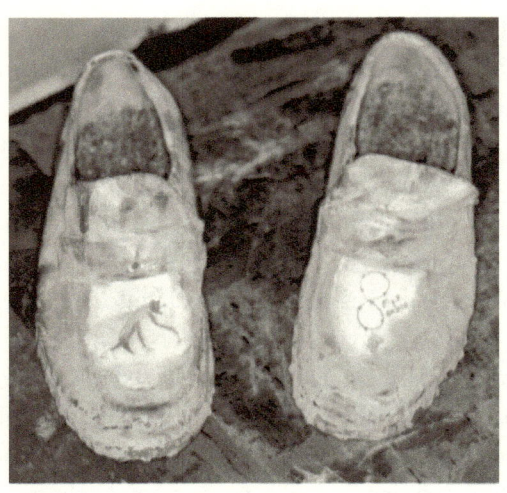

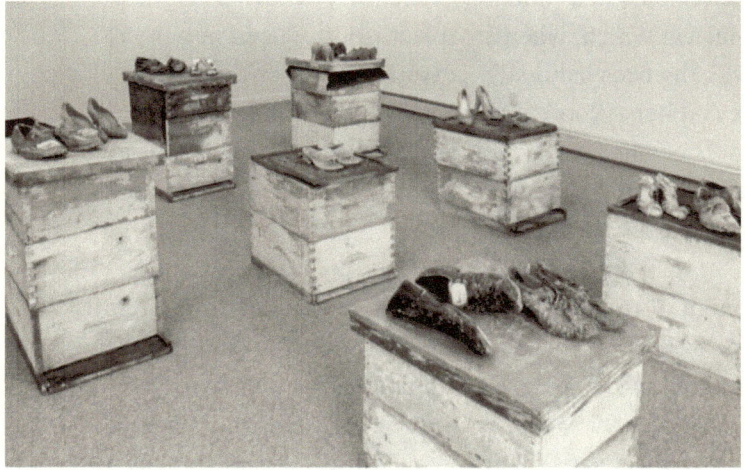

24. *Man's Shoes*, 1994
   photograph by William Eakin

25. *Dance Shoes and Hive Blankets*, 1992
   installation view at Strike 3 Gallery
   photograph by William Eakin

reminiscent of her works in *The Library* – as well as, in several cases, the addition of drawings she made while studying the bees. On the top of *Man's Shoes* (1994) there are two drawings embedded within the layers of wax. The first, seen on the right shoe, pictures the profile of a bee. The second, on the left shoe, is a diagram labeled as 'Fig. 8 Dance' that outlines a communication dance – specifically the waggle dance, which is performed by worker bees to communicate sources of nectar or pollen. Interestingly enough, the movements of a bee performing the waggle dance, which in the diagram are pictured as a figure eight, describe the space around the two half-circle tables of *Pocket Books for the Queen Bee*, in the centre of which the actual *waggling* would be performed. As we see, Dyck's initial move into working with the material world of bees – working with beeswax, studying the honeybees, placing object in the hive – also includes a corresponding move towards trying to understand what might be called the *habitus* of the bees.

This dual process, using human and other-than-human practices, points to the artist's desire not just to 'use' the bees as a medium but rather to produce work through a creative dialogue with the honeybees. This is apparent in her intensive research into the bees, which involved reading books, working with experts on bees and with beekeepers (including, among others, Mark L. Winston and Phil Veldhuis), as well as directly interacting with various hives. There is a profound respect evident in Dyck's relationship with these little beings. "My first visit to an apiary was like entering another world," she states, noting that she "stood in awe at the 50,000 moving beings" in the beehive, "a place filled with movement, scent, warmth, sound and ambrosia."[25] It is into this world that Dyck introduces the objects of her work, which become moments of dialogue between humans and bees, between the artist and the Queen Bee.

*

"When the beekeeper first showed me the Queen Bee as she was laying yet another of her 2000 eggs a day," Dyck tells us "a project titled 'The Extended Wedding Party' surfaced in my mind."[26] This elaborate installation is a key work in the artist's practice because it is here that we witness the overlapping of the two main perspectives that define her approach to art. On the one hand, this project centres on the exploration of objects related to a fundamental practice within the domestic and everyday lives of many people: the ritual celebration of marriage, the *wedding*. On the other hand, the material treatment of the works on display reflects her emerging vision of interspecies communication, with each object representing the site for a dialogue of discourses: human and other-than-human.

In fact, it is also with this installation that we see Dyck share the artist's spotlight with her little collaborators, whose creative processes – thanks to an ingenious set up – are literally present within the space of the exhibition. What underlies both of these approaches is the question of reproductive practices, centering on the roles of the bride in the human bonding ritual of the wedding and the Queen Bee in the procreative capacities of the beehive.

The overriding scheme of the show is, as the title indicates, the traditional wedding party. Walking amid the works in this installation we find representations of, among other, the groom, groomsman, flower girl, bridesmaid and, the focus of the project, the bride; in each case, the presence of the figure is denoted through

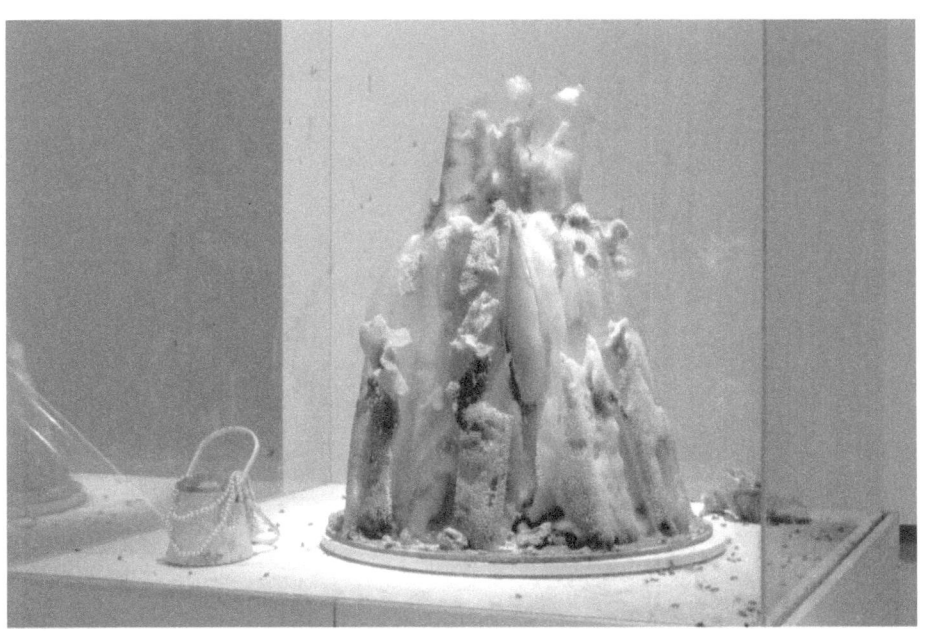

26. Honeybees working on *Lady in Waiting*, 1995
    installation view at Winnipeg Art Gallery
    photograph by Sheila Spence
    image courtesy Winnipeg Art Gallery

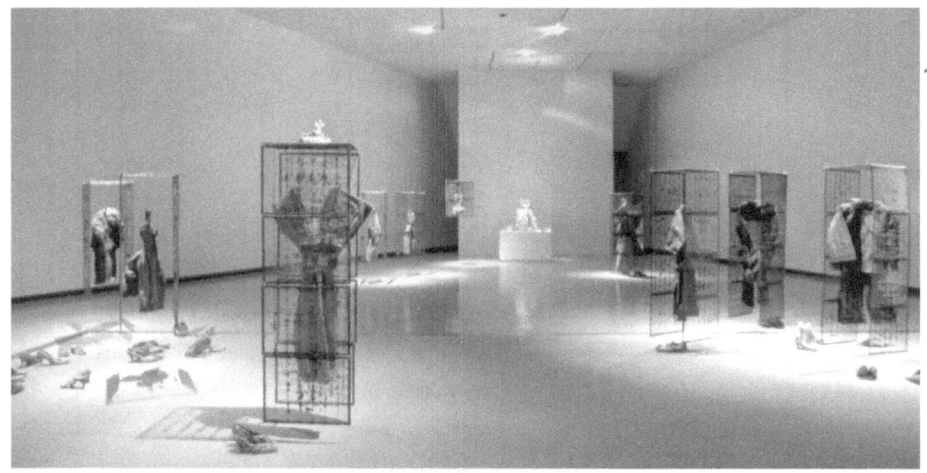

27. *Extended Wedding Party*, 1995
    installation view at Winnipeg Art Gallery
    photograph by Sheila Spence
    image courtesy Winnipeg Art Gallery

a specific mode of formal clothing, mostly – with the key exception of the bride's dress – made out of old hive blankets (used to keep beehives warm). These are sewn by a number of the artist's friends, women who "adapt their skills to an unfamiliar thick waterproofed fabric ... covered with cells, wax, resin" in order to, as Joan Borsa tells us, "transform the small innocuous blankets into elaborate, ornate, wedding garments."[27] These symbolic garments are displayed in modular cage-like metal racks, previously used in man-made beehives, which hang from the ceiling in intervals throughout the space. Individual items are contained yet easily visible, materially and spatially defined as separate object-oriented entities that are also components in a larger subjective system of cultural meanings and values.

    Within proximity of the hanging clothes are numerous pairs of shoes arranged on the floor, in some cases matched to specific garments and in others orphaned. It is interesting to note that there are more pairs of shoes than are necessary for the symbolic figures in this wedding party, suggesting on the level of the object Dyck's extension of the practical systems of behaviours – wearing specific types of clothing, standing and acting in particular ways in relation to the ceremonial space and to other participants, among others – related to this (human) ritual.

    Paired with this scheme is the creative practice of the honeybees, which physically and conceptually extends the parameters of the wedding party beyond its human limits. This is evident in the multiple applications of honeycomb and beeswax that adorn the various garments and accompanying accessories in the installation, decorating these items with a clearly other-than-human aesthetic. Remnants of the bees' work appear sporadically on the surfaces of the altered objects; sometimes it is highly visible – such as the multiple fragments within the structure of the metal racks and built up on the various shoes – and other times it is more subtle – like the material traces that have become part of the blankets and now the clothing of the wedding party. If we look closely at the two *Bridesmaid's Dresses* we see what the artist refers to as honeybee "embroidery," lines and patterns of honeycomb and beeswax that visually reflect the structural relationship between the bees and the beehive. This correlation is crucial since, similar to the way the clothing infers the presence of the bridesmaids, Dyck's adaptation of the hive blankets denotes the presence of the bees through the vestiges of their material histories.

Accompanying these two hanging bridesmaids dresses are matching pairs of wax-covered, blue high-heeled shoes, which have beeswax sculpted flowers attached to the back and tops of each. These bee-altered shoes directly relate to Dyck's earlier series, which (as discussed above) included both bee and human alterations. Much of the footwear in this installation, in fact, appears to be adapted from this preceding group of works – the groom, for example, seems to be wearing *Man's Shoes* with the figure eight on the top. If previously these shoes were presented as stand-alone objects, such as in her exhibition *Danced Shoes and Hive Blankets* where they sit in pairs on top of hive boxes, in *The Extended Wedding Party* they participate in a larger, integrated production that more fully addresses the hybrid nature of Dyck's approach.

There is a back-and-forth between the clothes and shoes that defines the interconnected nature of the figures in this wedding ceremony, one that reflects and is put into dialogue with the interrelated behaviours of the honeybees within a functioning hive. As Borsa states: "Aganetha Dyck's work seems to follow bees to the limit of human

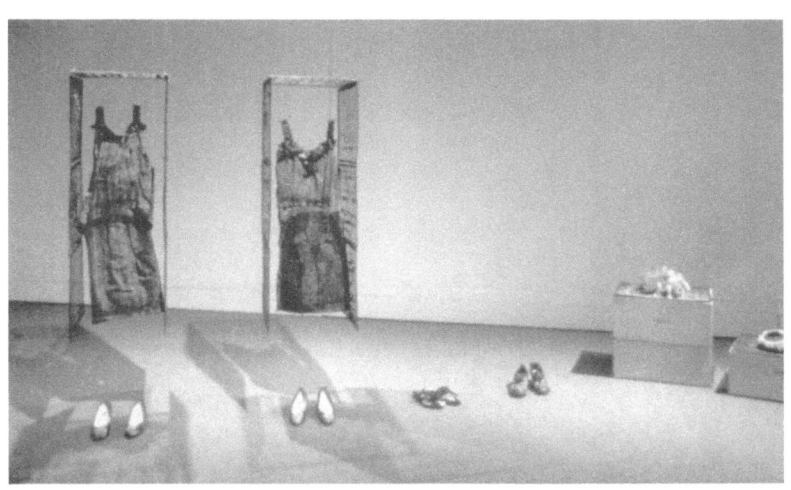

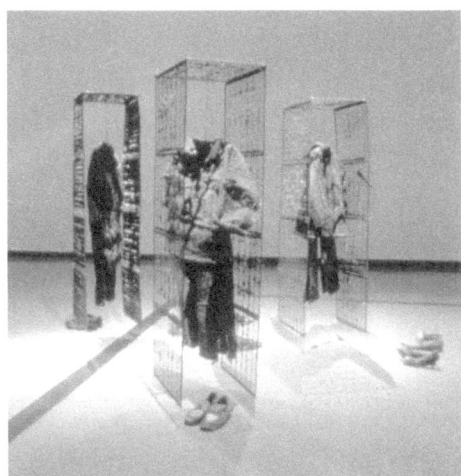

28. *Extended Wedding Party* [detail of *Bridesmaid's Dresses*], 1995

29. *Extended Wedding Party* [detail of *Groom*], 1995
    installation view at Winnipeg Art Gallery
    photograph by Sheila Spence
    image courtesy Winnipeg Art Gallery

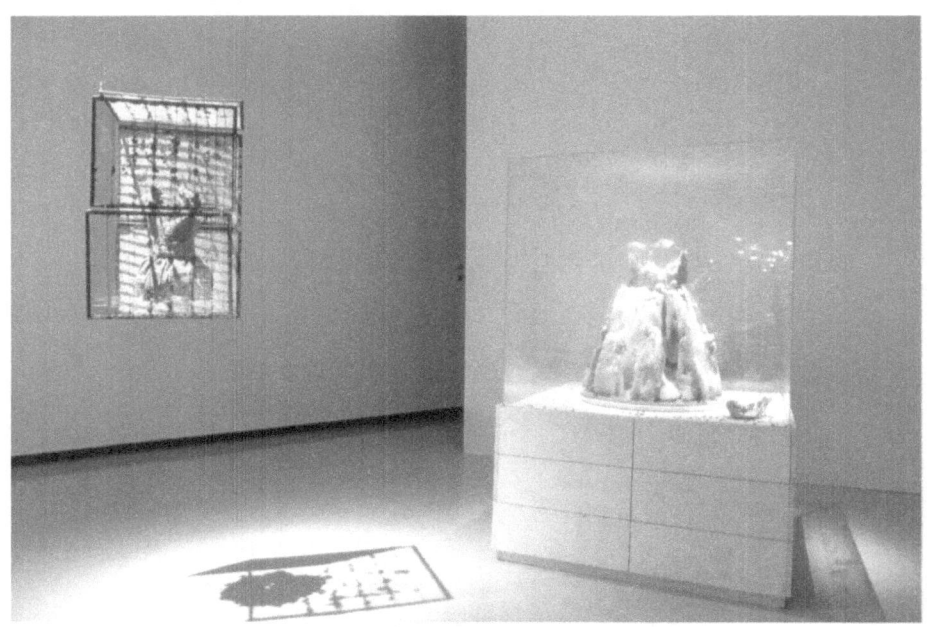

30. *Extended Wedding Party* [detail of *Flower Girl* and *Bride*], 1995
installation view at Winnipeg Art Gallery
photograph by Sheila Spence
image courtesy Winnipeg Art Gallery

understanding."[28] Yet, I would suggest that by facing up to human limitations, and correspondingly embracing the possibilities inherent in the creative practice of the bees, Dyck is postulating a new conceptual and visual territory. The resulting hybrid aesthetic materially embodies a fundamental overlap between the two alternative or even parallel systems of habits, with the human ritual of the wedding being adapted to the world of bees and the practice of the honeybees being adapted to the world of human rituals.

Reflecting the traditional wedding structure, in the installation at the Winnipeg Art Gallery the bridesmaids dresses are presented with the maid of honor's dress, all of which stand alongside the bride. However, this powerfully female-oriented group is located at the front of a long, telescoping gallery space that we approach by moving through the rest of the figures – as if walking down an aisle. Thus, the bride takes the position of prominence usually occupied by the groom, who instead is found off to one side with two groomsmen; this reversal means, simply put, the groom is required to move towards the bride and be *given away* to her. Such an arrangement, with the bride at the centre of all the activities, objects and processes that define this marriage practice, mirrors the role of the Queen Bee at the core of the social behaviours in a hive.

And it is this bride-Queen that dominates the entire installation with her magnificent presence. Much of the scholarship on this project focuses on the *Glass Dress: Lady in Waiting* (1992-1998), an undersized glass wedding dress onto which the bees have built undulating layers of honeycomb that defines the full, flowing skirt. "The wedding dress is intensely sensual as the bees have abstractly arranged the wax in folds resembling a fantasy landscape of cascades and mountains," Elizabeth Martin

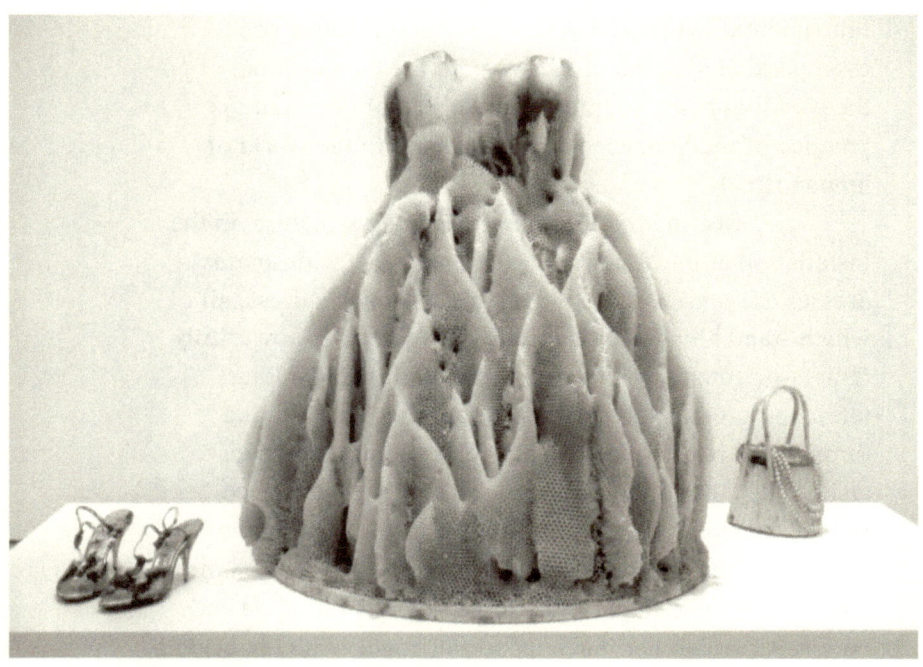

31. *Glass Dress: Lady in Waiting*, 1992-1998
    installation view at the National Gallery of Canada
    image courtesy National Gallery of Canada

and Vivian Meyer tell us.[29] Displayed inside a Plexiglas box, this dress is accompanied by a pair of bee-altered high-heeled shoes and handbag with a pearl necklace draped overtop – objects that recall Dyck's earlier projects with the bees.

Also inside this Plexiglas box are numerous living bees, which, for the duration of the exhibition, were housed in beehives located in the white plinth on which the work was situated; the bees were able to leave the space of the gallery through a tube, allowing them to collect the natural materials (nectar, pollen) necessary to continue building honeycomb into the dress. This living quality – a powerful element, full of sounds and smells – enhanced the interspecies aspect of the installation, making the Bride's *Glass Dress*, in Borsa's words, "a spectacle, resplendent yet eerie, the centerpiece of a strange three-dimensional still life. As the bees industriously animate the glass form (the bride's dress), the intricate honeycomb structures evolve – an organic architecture, a focused potent energy within the otherwise lifeless, skeletal remains of the staged wedding pageantry."[30]

The resulting dress, as Juan Antonio Ramirez describes it, "is a fascinating creation with a disturbing beauty: the transparency of the glass, somewhat dimmed by the waxen varnish, produces an interesting dialogue between materials and textures." Ramirez even compares Dyck's bride to the "glass bride" of Duchamp's *The Bride Stripped Bare by Her Bachelors, Even* (1923), better known as *The Large Glass*.[31] The parallels are striking and add an historical dimension to the bride-Queen, who can be seen as an extension of a number of the qualities of Duchamp's bride. Foremost among these is the notion of mechanical movements (behaviours), central in Duchamp's complex schema for this work, which defines a specific relationship between, in the case of *The Large Glass*, the bachelors and the bride they are attempting to 'strip bare' – revealing the bride as desiring-machine, a motor that blossoms from a virgin into a bride.

Yet, whereas these (habitual) movements are suggested through Duchamp's abstract visual system, Dyck makes them an actual functioning element within the work by, in its original installation, including a living colony of honeybees (with virgin-workers, bachelor-drones and a bride-Queen) who produce the sculptural bride-Queen during the exhibition. As a response to Duchamp's *delay in glass*, as he describes his *Large Glass*, Dyck's *Lady in Waiting* draws attention to the manner in which this bride-Queen is materially engaged in an "indecisive reunion" that must literally wait for the ritual-like processes of the bees before *The Extended Wedding Party* can be fulfilled.[32]

*

In concert with her major survey exhibition at the Winnipeg Art Gallery in 1995, Dyck developed the outdoor installation *Sports Night in Canada* at the St. Norbert Arts and Cultural Centre. This parallel project is a virtual reversal of what we experience in *The Extended Wedding Party*; as opposed to bringing the honeybees into the gallery space (safely contained of course), in this case it is the human spectator that is relocated into the space of the bees, into the zone of their apiary.

"I am very excited about this apiary/gallery space," Dyck tells Gilles Hébert, Director of St. Norbert Arts & Cultural Centre, "The bees and I will create the artwork. I will be the curator and the tour guide, the bees will be the guards. The visitors to this gallery will have to dress for beekeeping."³³ Considered as both apiary and outdoor gallery, this space celebrates human and other-than-human creative practices in a way that highlights and challenges the possibilities inherent in this relationship. It is not just Dyck who has to negotiate with these little creators, we must also be willing and prepared – in this gallery we dress as beekeepers – to experience the entire creative being of the honeybees. Here we no longer encounter these co-creators through the evidence of their work, or, as with the presentation of *Lady in Waiting*, separated by a museum-style Plexiglas box, but instead must face the power of these small beings directly within their own environment.

      The installation itself is comprised of the wooden beehive boxes and their many inhabitants, and the series of pieces of equipment from numerous sports (hockey, baseball, football, fencing) that Dyck gives to the bees for alteration. This group of works has an obvious connection with her *Hockey Night in Canada* series, in which she used the natural qualities of wool to produce a number of shrunken toques. She extends this engagement with the natural by placing sports equipment within the beehives, handing over control of the transformation of the object to the bees. "Honeybees will hang comb from any object put into their hives," Mark L. Winston points out, a habit that Dyck uses "to collaborate with her bee partners" by encouraging them to do what they do naturally.³⁴

      In this respect Dyck becomes the *curator* of the works in this outdoor apiary/gallery. She selects and arranges objects with the space, while allowing the honeybees to use this readymade sports equipment as the basis for their own sculptural interventions. And the beekeeper Phil Veldhuis is the tour guide who lifts each

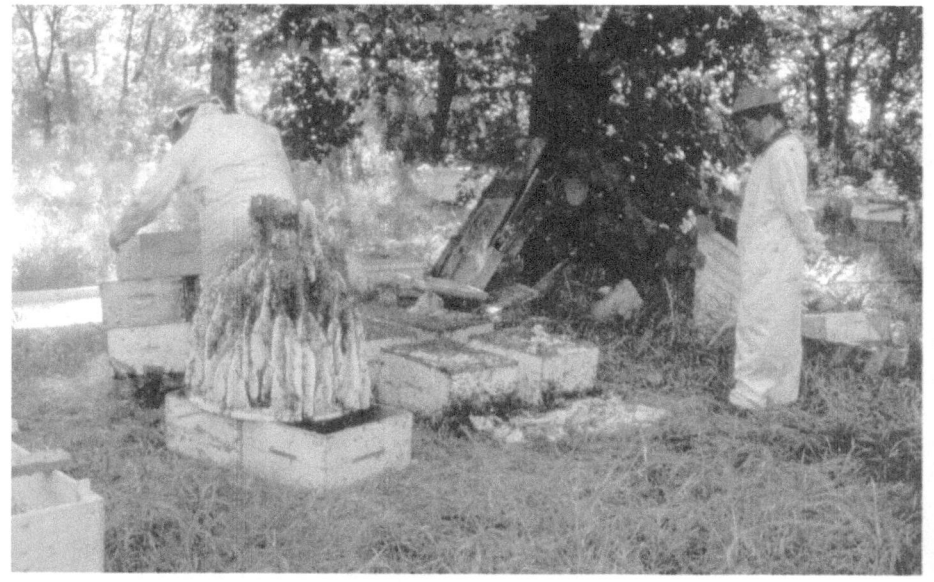

32. Dyck, Phil Veldhuis and Di Brandt removing *Glass Dress* from bee hive, 1995
    installation view at St. Norbert Arts and Cultural Centre Apiary
    photograph by Peter Dyck

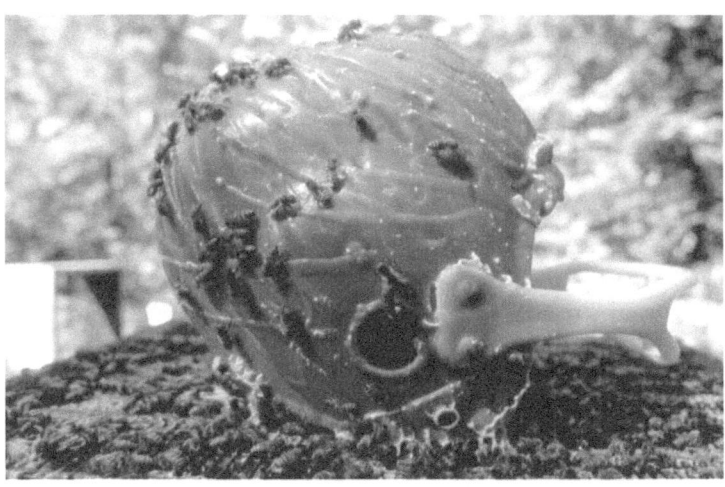

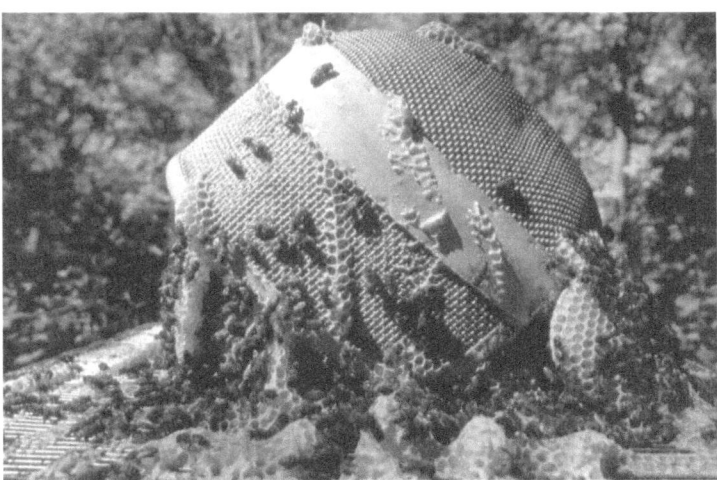

33. Honeybees working on *Sports Night in Canada* [football helmet], 1995

34. Honeybees working on *Sports Night in Canada* [fencing mask], 1995 installation view at St. Norbert Arts and Cultural Centre Apiary
photographs by William Eakin

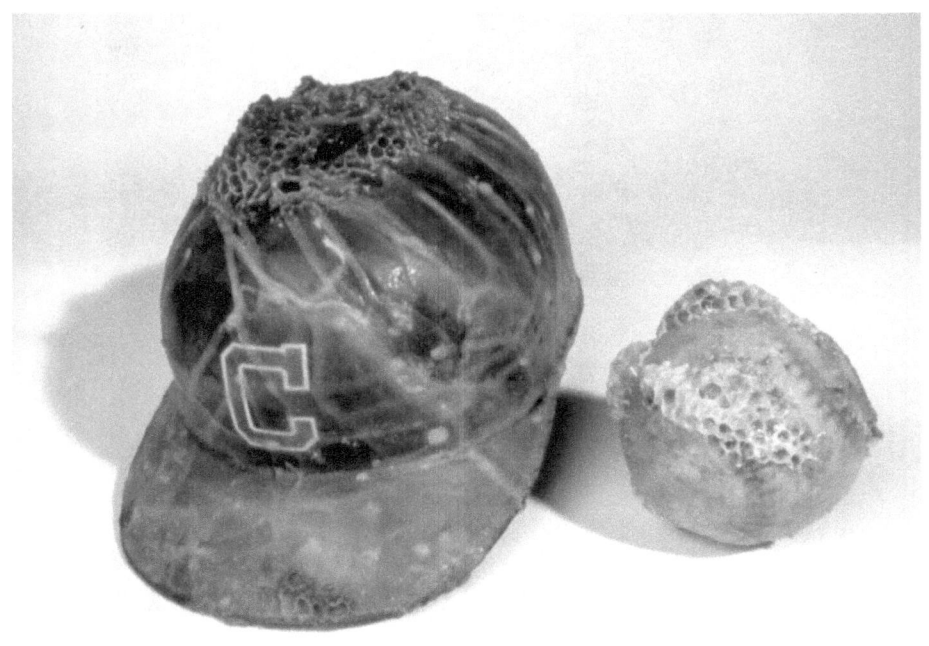

35. *Sports Night in Canada* [baseball hat and ball], 1995
photograph by Peter Dyck

hive lid for viewers, and calms both honeybees and viewers while explaining and answering many questions regarding honeybees. In terms of this collaboration, it is important to note that Peter and Richard Dyck prepared the apiary gallery site within a sunny forest clearing on the grounds of the St. Norbert Arts and Cultural Centre. In addition, the Centre's staff used a tractor to move long, thick fallen trees to act as bleachers for viewers afraid to go near the hives. A few binoculars were available for the viewers sitting on the woodland 'bleachers'.

We see the manner in which the bees construct honeycomb that almost completely covers the surface of several football helmets or decorates patches on the fencing mask, filling much of the interior space of these pieces of headgear. A layer of beeswax is visible on the baseball cap with honeycomb built around the top and brim; the accompanying ball is heavily encrusted – a photograph captures the bees as they work on this baseball. Some of these works, such as the red football shoulder pads and the Winnipeg Jets hockey stick (with pucks hidden inside the mass of comb), the bees built the honeycomb onto the object and the grate of the hives – Dyck exhibits these within gallery spaces on top of the accompanying beehive boxes.

By turning St. Norbert Arts & Cultural Centre into an apiary/gallery space, Dyck, with the help of beekeeper Phil Veldhuis, provided an opportunity for visitors to witness firsthand the creation of her "beeswax work in the location where much of it was produced."[35] As part of her attempts to activate the space as a type of gallery, she gave tours of *Sports Night in Canada* to the groups of people who came to the site, unearthing the works-in-progress for all to see – with the bees continuing to work before everyone's eyes. In one case, Dyck tells me, a blind man wearing shorts and short-sleeved shirt asked to

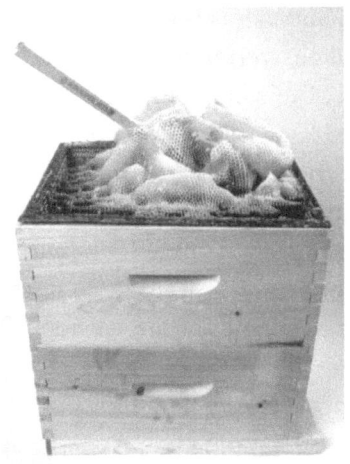

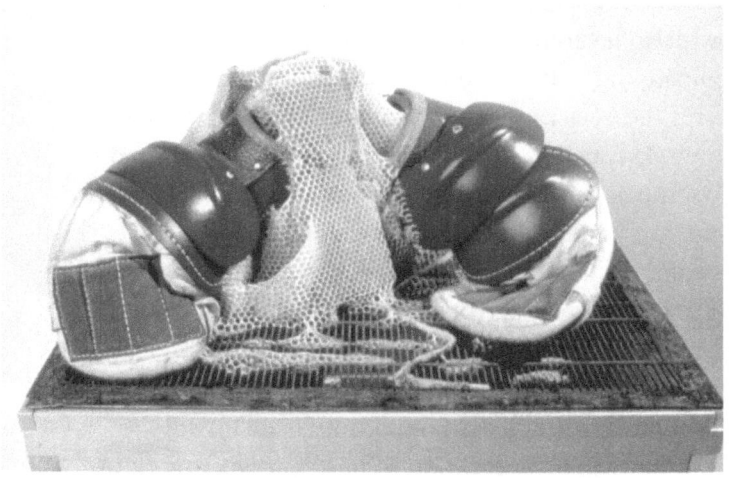

36. *Sports Night in Canada* [hockey stick and pucks], 1995

37. *Sports Night in Canada* [football shoulder pads], 1995
    images courtesy of Aganetha Dyck

be taken to the bees; while she hesitated (wearing a full bee suit), Dyck eventually took him over to the specific beehive he requested:

> after lifting the lid of the beehive with a sports helmet inside ... he asked me if I ever allowed the honeybees to give my hands a massage. No, never was my reply. He asked me to remove my gloves, I did and he took my hand and gently placed my palm over thousands of honeybees working on the helmet. He did the same procedure with his hand and talked to me about honeybees and their importance to the world. No, he never kept bees. Then he asked to go back to his guide and they left. I was so stunned by this experience. I never got his name, nor the name of the guide. I just stood there wondering what just occurred.[36]

Encounters such as this suggest the full range of relational and embodied exchanges that occur behind the veil of beeswax on Dyck's sculptures. These tours allowed people to engage with the apiary environment, to experience part of what Dyck experiences when creating her bee works.

While it is easy to look at the honeycomb on the baseball and imagine all the bees that made it possible, it is another thing to watch as the comb is built wall by wall, cell by cell. One of the crucial elements of Dyck's approach to art is her interest in and even need for the incorporation of process into the practice of creating. In the site-specific exhibition of *Sports Night in Canada* she actively opened up her relationship with the bees and their environment, including the apiary and beekeepers who aid in her work, inviting us to be part of her exploration of the habits and consciousness of these little creative beings.

Moments of Interspecies Communication

Aganetha Dyck's work with the bees marks an important development not just in her own artistic practice, but also in Canadian art more generally. The reasons for this are numerous and, in many respects, still being determined. While the unique and challenging aesthetics of her bee works are widely discussed, the ways her practice participates in critical debates around art, science and environmentalism has taken on more urgency within the literature on her work. "The honeybees taught me to understand that I was part of the global environment," she tells me, a powerful statement that calls attention to the scope of her project.

What is at stake in Dyck's visual research into the bees can be summed up in a key concept that she employs: *interspecies communication*. We have encountered this idea briefly when discussing relations between human and other-than-human beings, but it is important to consider it in more depth. This idea of communications among different species, such as between humans and bees – and equally between bees and humans – is seen as a way of thinking through the possibility of understanding and sharing meanings within the world, from different but complimentary points of view. We see this in *The Extended Wedding Party*, where Dyck presents the overlapping repetitive or ritualistic schemas of the Queen Bee and the Bride as a single visual utterance, documenting the potential for a meaningful interaction through the overlapping discourses associated with these powerful female figures. In *Bee Time: Lessons from the Hive* Mark L. Winston describes her art as "the dialogue we would like to have with bees if we could only find a common language."[37] Such a quest is not simply a curiosity for Dyck, who instead treats the development of interspecies communication as a cultural imperative that is directly linked to environmental questions of global survival, not just of humans but all beings on the planet.

"As an artist, I continue to question what my research into interspecies communication suggests or where it might lead to."[38] Following her experimentations in *The Extended Wedding Party* and *Sports Night in Canada*, especially the bringing together of the worlds of humans and bees into a hybrid space, her work begins more actively to address this concept through a play of realities. Through her work Dyck will *attempt* – an important word that shows up prominently in her exhibition titled *Inter Species Communication Attempt and Attempt with Conversation: two hives speaking to one another* – to communicate both with the bees and the human viewer who engages with them, presenting overlapping visions that draw attention to the possibilities of shared meanings.

This exploration represents the basis of her practice from this point to the present, including, I suggest, the works Dyck has created after becoming severely allergic to bee stings; in these post-bee works the need for interspecies communication is in fact heightened as her collaboration is necessarily performed at a distance, both physical and emotional. What these later projects with the bees share is a desire not to limit the scope of her practice to questions

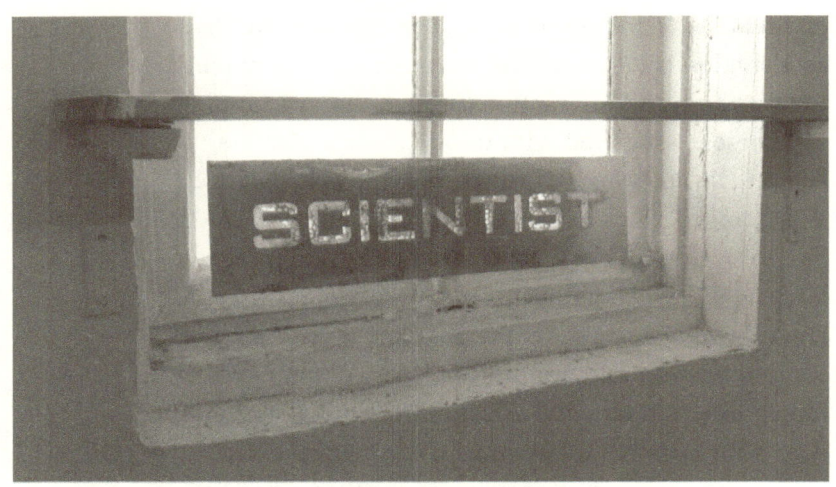

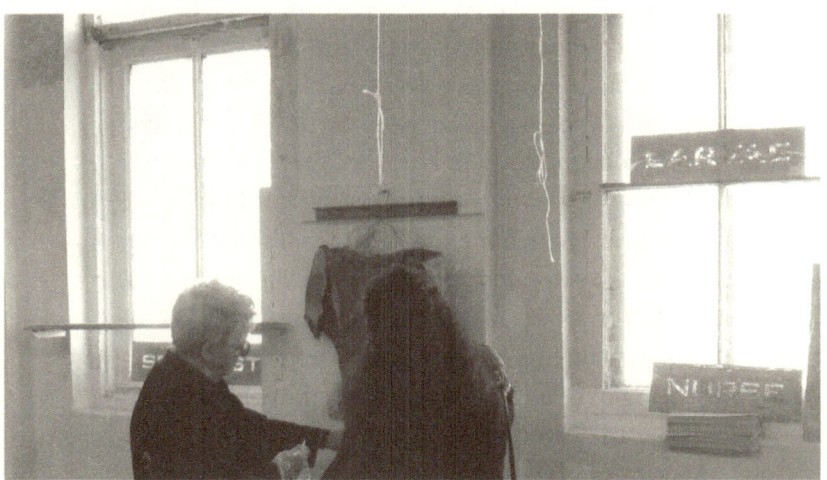

38. *Scientist*, 2007-2008
    view in Dyck's studio

39. View of three *Signs* in Dyck's studio, 2010

of human creativity and presence in the world, but instead to locate her research in a more radical reconsideration of the play of becoming-creative that is shared by humans and other-than-humans alike.

*

In her 2009 exhibition at the Burnaby Art Gallery, titled *Collaborations*, Dyck brings together several series of works that examine the concept of 'communication' from different perspectives. Earlier I discussed my encounter with works from one of these projects, the series of *Eleven Signs*, which I saw during my visit to the artist's studio. Each of these signs is an acute materialization of human language, with cut-outs of single words associated with the care and study of bees ("queen," "drone," "worker," "egg," "pupae," "larvae," "nurse," "hive," "beekeeper," "scientist," "artist"), which are given to the bees who apply their own material language to them. Dyck begins with basic building blocks of communication: words, which become part of a more expansive signifying system that references meanings for the experiences of both humans and bees. This is the foundation for a mode of *trans-species perception*[39] – a concept that allows us to question the limits of what is communicable by extending the accepted parameters of experiencing the world.

Such a change must involve rethinking the dominant paradigms that define the idea of perceiving, which in turn affects how and what we communicate – as well as who we can communicate with. Throughout Dyck's work with the bees she continually pushes the boundaries of the communicable, trying to share with these little beings a sense of what it means to experience the world from their perspective. In an attempt to outdo her own limitations and consider a more broad sense of the scope of human perception and communication, for her series *Working in the Dark* she works with the tactile writing system of Braille to create works that move beyond a strict sense of sight.

Developed in 1824 by the blind Frenchman Louis Braille, this system allows people to read by touching a series of 6-dot cells with one's fingers; letters, numbers, punctuation marks and words can be communicated through this code of dots and spaces. Dyck's use of this mode of communication in her project reflects a number of key elements about the bees that interest her, including the tactility of the hive as a living environment. There is also a material connection between these two systems, albeit an arbitrary one: they are both constructed out of cells, with the Braille alphabet consisting of 6-dots and honeycomb units made with 6 sides (you work with both *in the dark*). Such a synchronicity is important for Dyck, since it functions through connections that are not strictly logical and therefore creatively point to a space beyond human logic, a space of *becoming-other-than-human*.

Another element that interested Dyck was the historical relationship between Braille as writing system for the blind and the 19th century blind beekeeper Francis Huber, whose 1814 book *New Observation Upon Bees* had a direct impact on the works that comprise *Working in the Dark*. "In publishing my observations upon honeybees, I will not conceal the fact that it was not with my own eyes that I made them," Huber wrote in the preface to his text with the help of his servant and collaborator, Francis Burnens.[40] The idea of observing the bees not through sight but rather as an experience of touch, smell, sound and discussion is taken literally by Dyck, who decides to give a text to the bees in Braille, a

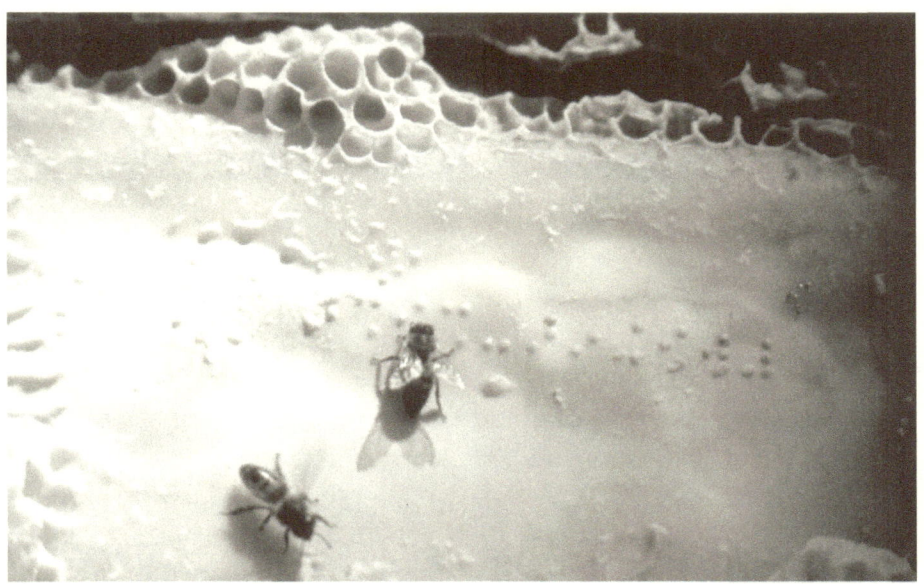

40. Honeybees working on first line of the Braille poem
for *Working in the Dark*, 1999
photograph by William Eakin

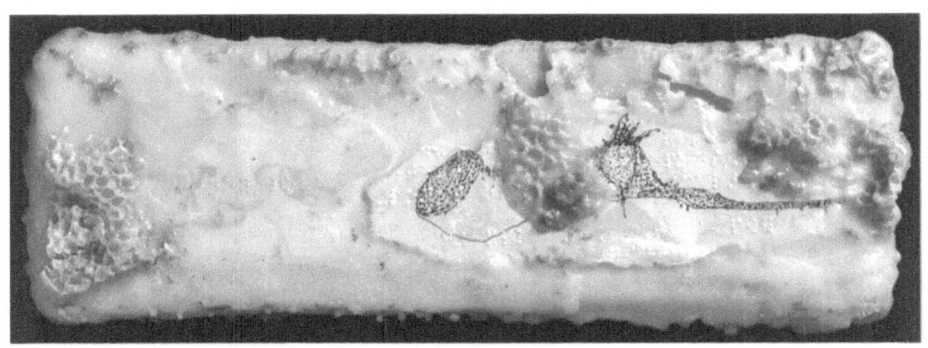

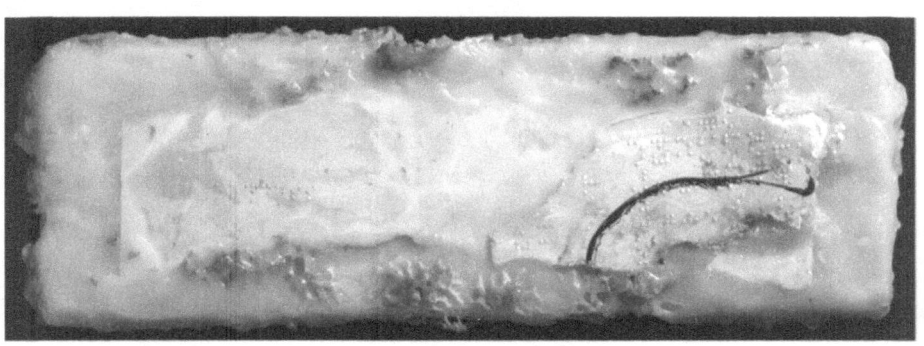

41-42. *Poem to the Bees by Di Brandt* [two lines of the poem], 2007-2008

system of communication they can interact with in their own natural ways.

For this project Dyck commissioned the Canadian poet Di Brandt to write a poem specifically addressed to the bees. "How do you write for bees?" Brandt asks, "This was the intriguing, disturbing, exciting question Aganetha posed for me when she decided to extend her multimedia cross-species collaboration to include human written text."[41] Brandt proceeds to consider an entire cosmology of the bees, at once natural and scientific, real and poetic, imagining their world and trying to make herself part of it through her words.

The resulting fifty-four line poem, which begins with the wonderful phrase "& then everything goes bee," was transcribed into Braille. Each line is presented on its own sheet of paper, which also include several of Dyck's drawings of her studies of bees, all of which are waxed onto small wooden boards. These fifty-four works were then given to the honeybees, placed into the hive, where they were 'read' by the bees who then re-inscribed their own material language overtop. In her text Brandt quotes Dyck as describing Braille as "a language of dots the bees will surely know how to read, because they too make dots on surfaces every time they begin a new honeycomb, and touch them over and over in the darkness of the hive with their hands/feet."[42]

"Who knows," Brandt continues, "what the bees will do with the poem after they've read it? Or what they will want to say or write back to us?"[43] Dyck attempts to answer these questions by sharing the results of her work with a group of blind viewers during a tour of *Inter Species Communication* at Gallery One One One, who were invited to *read* the material differences in what the text communicates. After reading the original Braille

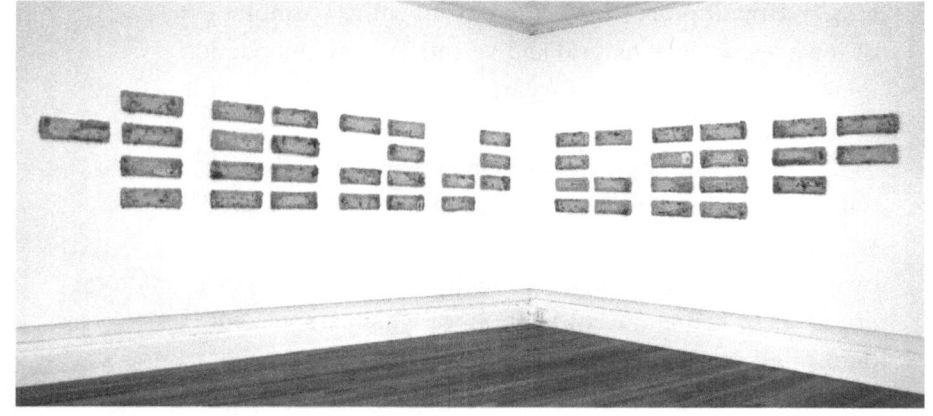

43. *Poem to the Bees by Di Brandt*, 2007-2008
 installation view at Burnaby Art Gallery

transcription, the viewers then tried to read the bee-altered poem with some humorous results. Interestingly, as they pointed out to Dyck, the standard Braille dot and the beeswax anchor dot created by the honeybees – used, as mentioned above, to indicate where new honeycomb will be built – are the same size. While the final text is of course illegible, for us as much as a blind viewer, it nonetheless speaks to an understanding of communication pushed beyond its practical (logical) limits into new conceptual and visual territories.

*

Up to now the question of communication has been treated as somewhat direct, with Dyck housing a hive of bees in an art gallery, bringing viewers to an apiary and giving the honeybees words or texts to alter in either written or Braille form. This directness, however, begins to give way to a more mediated treatment of interspecies communication in *Hive Scans*, a collaborative project created with her son, the media artist Richard Dyck – a series also presented in the exhibition *Collaborations*.

    Originally consisting of 17 large-scale photographic images of the darkened interior world of the bees (more scans have been subsequently added to the series), these works are the result of physically placing a digital scanner into the hive and repeatedly creating scans of the space and activities of the bees as captured through this device. What we see is not a realistic photographic rendering but rather abstract digital traces in which we witness both the environment of the beehive and the image capturing technology itself.

    Along with the fragments of hive and flashes of stilled and moving bees – and the occasional glimpses of the objects Dyck placed in the hive – we see the light of the scanner at different moments as it moves through the space, including distortions caused by the device's inability to properly communicate these visually obscured scenes. This can be readily seen in the disjointed images of bees presented throughout this series. As Robin Laurence describes:

> The bees themselves register as streaks and smears of brown and gold, as slightly blurred ovoid forms, or as highly resolved individuals, all their parts clearly articulated in the image-making moment. In some cases, they fly past the scanner or land on it and start depositing wax. They are shown massed around the alien objects or carefully tending the glowing hexagonal cells in which eggs, pupae or larvae may be developing.[44]

Within these *abstract landscapes*, as Laurence describes the photographic images, the bees are defined in their acts of becoming. But it is important not to forget that the picturing of these actions is communicated indirectly through the technological device of the scanner, which plays an active role in how the bees look in the images. For this reason, the bees appear in a manner that is beyond the modes of envisioning available through the human eye, a multi-chronotopic image that brings to mind other-than-human ways of perceiving the world.

In several cases we see repeated white lines that stutter across the picture plane, appearing as 'mistakes' – common when using scanners – that disrupt the visual information of the image itself. However, the artists' inclusion of these technological "errors" point to a desire for a different approach to

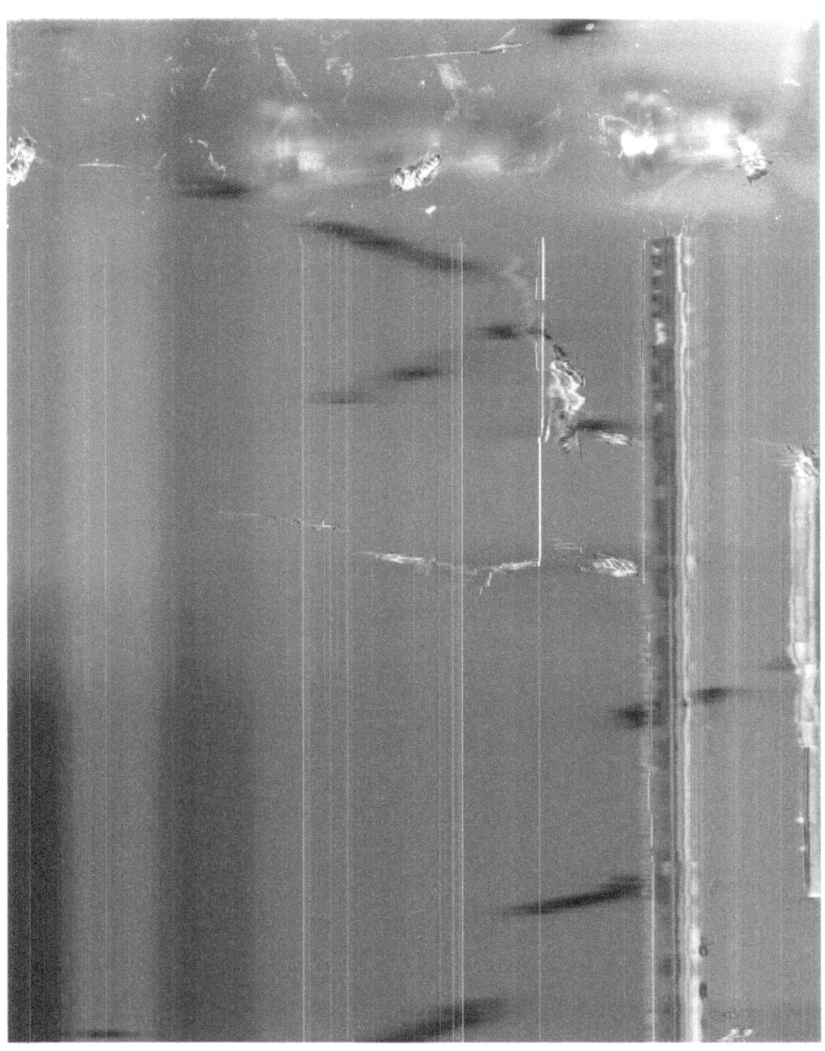

44. *Hive Scan*, 2001-2003
    collaboration between Aganetha and Richard Dyck

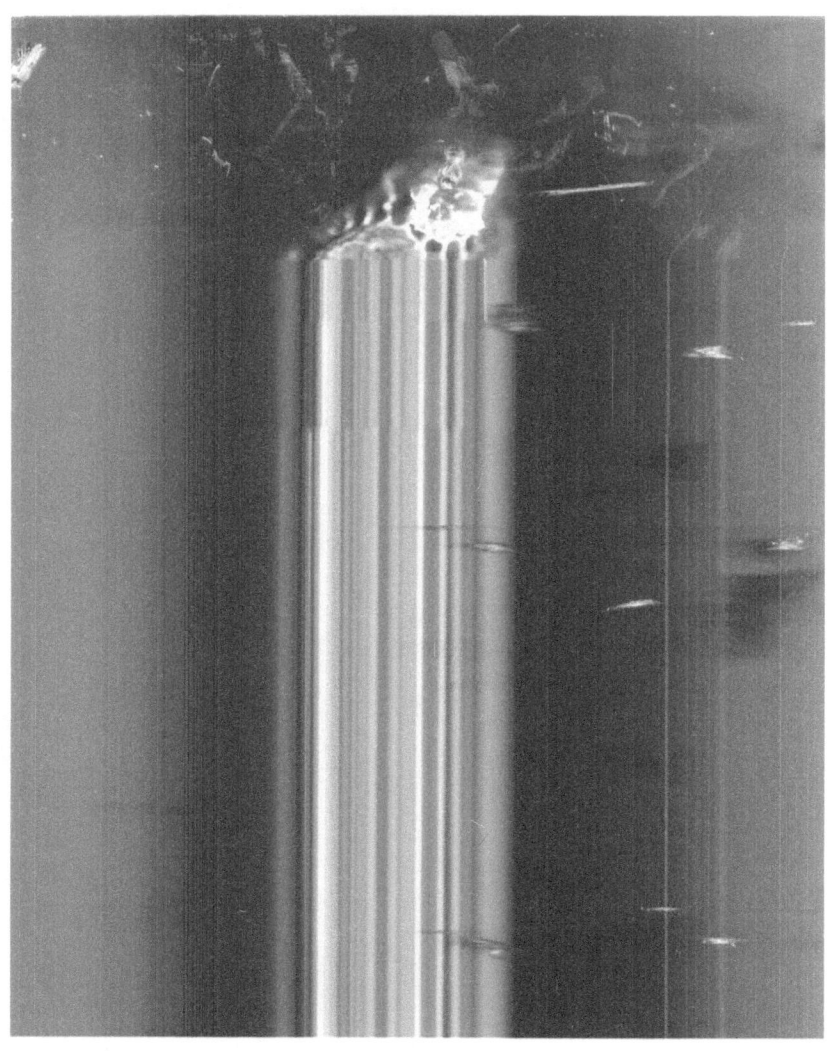

45. *Hive Scan*, 2001-2003
    collaboration between Aganetha and Richard Dyck

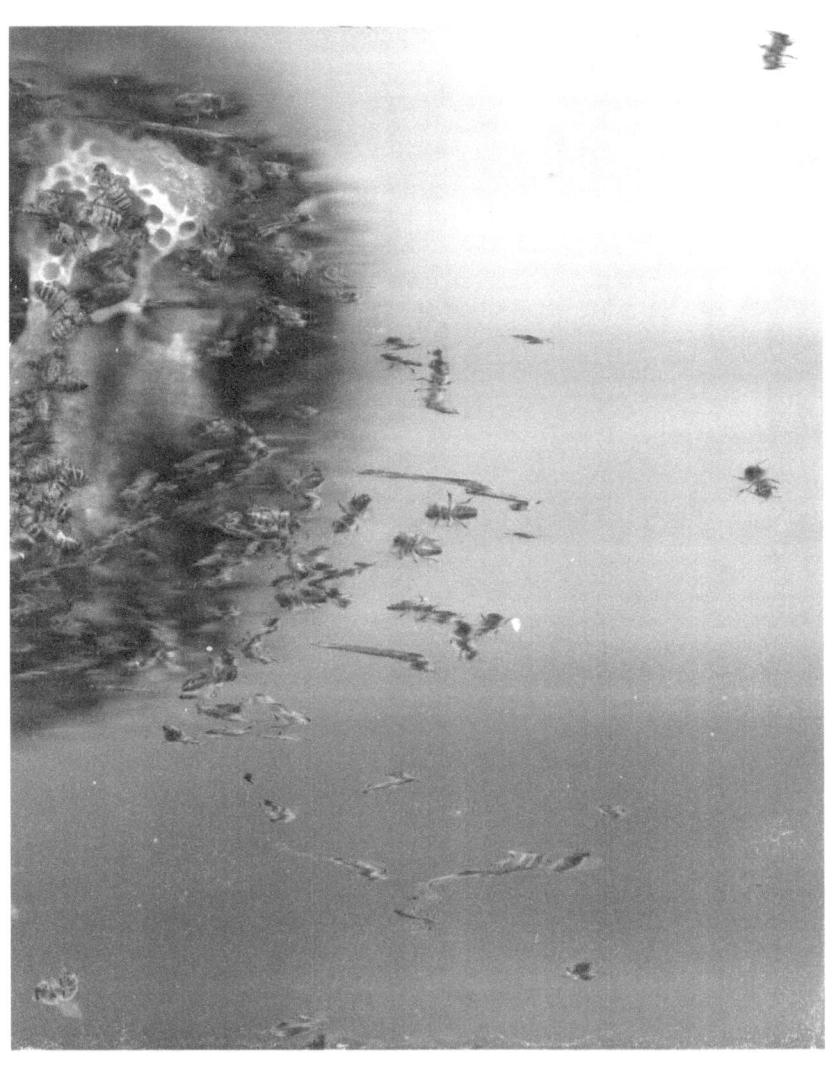

46. *Hive Scan*, 2001-2003
   collaboration between Aganetha and Richard Dyck

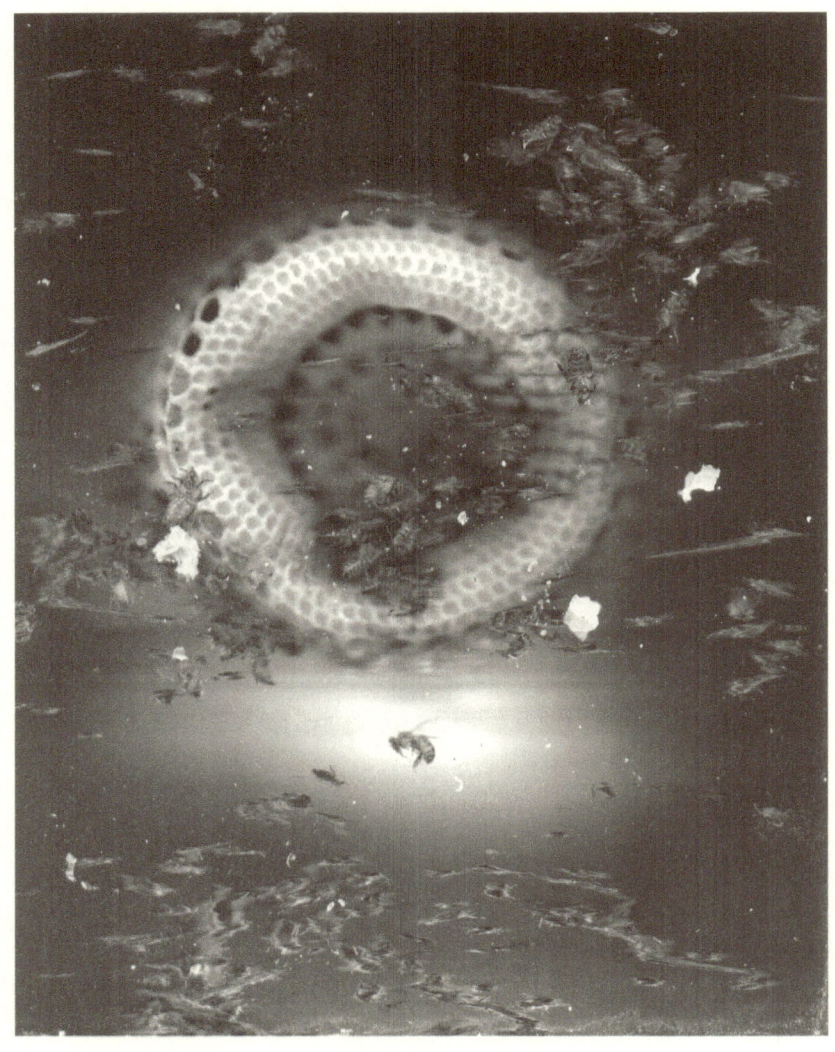

47. *Hive Scan*, 2001-2003
    collaboration between Aganetha and Richard Dyck

and understanding of representation, one that is neither strictly rational or functional, but rather pushes the limits of what is possible. This is a prerequisite to any honest attempt at interspecies communication: to see past our own limitations when viewing the world. These digital apparitions make us aware of our indirect relationship with the bees and, more importantly, that any communication between our species must be undertaken with this perceptual mediation in mind.

It is not enough to simply translate the world of the bees into a language we understand, since this will necessarily favour elements that reflect our views, our sense of being. The profound privileging of human sight, central to the advancement of photographic and digital technologies, tends to prejudice us against recognizing the significance of other senses that are dominant for a great many animals and insects. Honeybees, for example, "not only possess one of the most intricate chemical communication systems in the social insects, but also have evolved a dance language unparalleled in its ability to communicate the location of food resources and nest sites."[45] This is an alternative way of being in the world based within a form of knowing that is quite literally beyond human perception. How can we imagine this way of being? In *Hive Scans* Aganetha and Richard Dyck render not just a sense of the similarities or differences in our perceptions, but rather the possibility of finding ways of seeing that we can share with the bees, of finding a vision of the world that reflects both human and other-than-human forms of knowledge.

*

One of the enchanting qualities of *Hive Scans* is the otherworldliness of the images, which picture a surreal space beyond strict understandings of realism and abstraction. Moments of recognition punctuate the otherwise incommunicable expanse of these large photographs, in which the living quality of the bees is at once realistic (all too real in some respects) and painfully unrecognizable. This quality haunts Dyck's later artworks, especially her post-bee works that are the creative materialization of working through her inability to be in contact with these little beings – because of her newly developed allergy to bee stings. It also haunts the artist's relationship with her extended practice, which, at the time I met her, was in a transitional state. As a result of this necessary distance from direct interaction with the bees, we see a profound focus on mediation that I argue begins with *Hive Scans* and continues to be developed in her current works.

We must understand that Dyck's engagement with mediation, in addition to being a necessity of her later material practice, is a core concept for her approach to questions of ecology and her artistic attempts at communications among different species. More generally, we can recognize in these recent works a play with mediating one's environment and habitus that has remained a consistent approach for Dyck, in which the creative act represents a vital moment of rethinking distinctions between subject and world – between human and nature, human and technology, human and other-than-human. This is the basis for her vision of *interspecies communication* as moments of creative mediation.

The strange beauty of *Hive Scans* is directly connected with the multitude of meditational moments captured, the reality of which is embedded in the indirectness of the image. Again, these are not photo-realistic representations of beehive interiors but imperfect

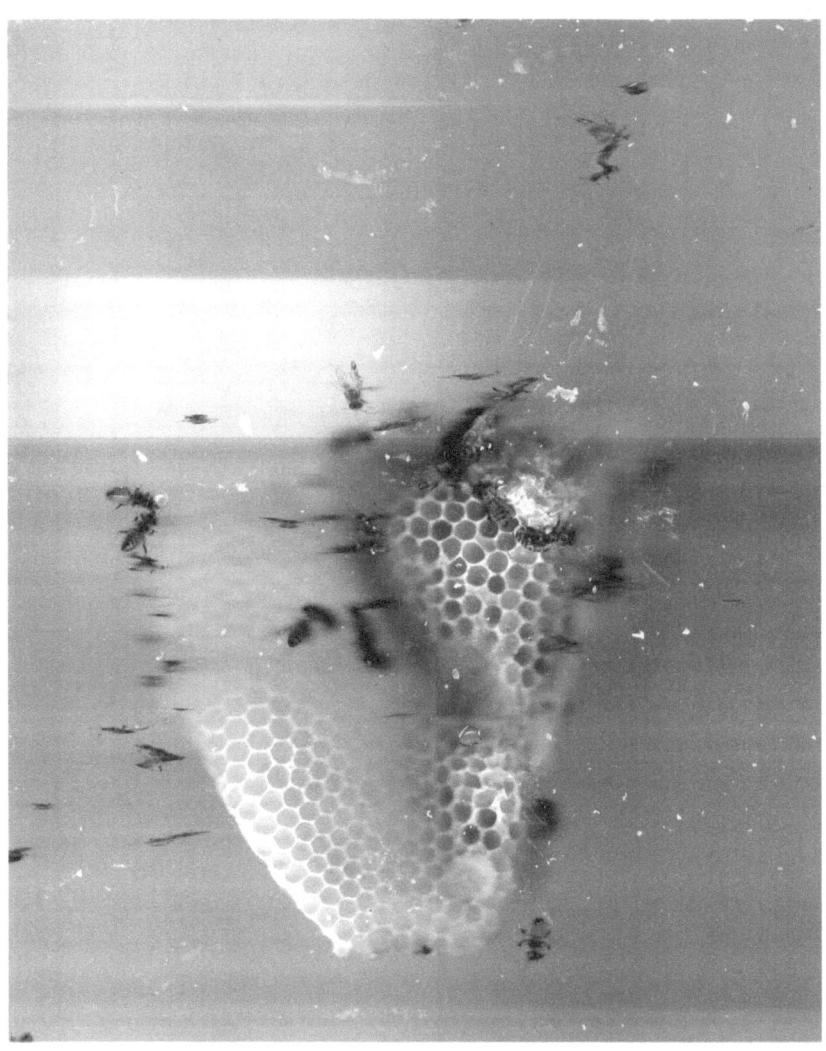

48. *Hive Scan*, 2001-2003
 collaboration between Aganetha and Richard Dyck

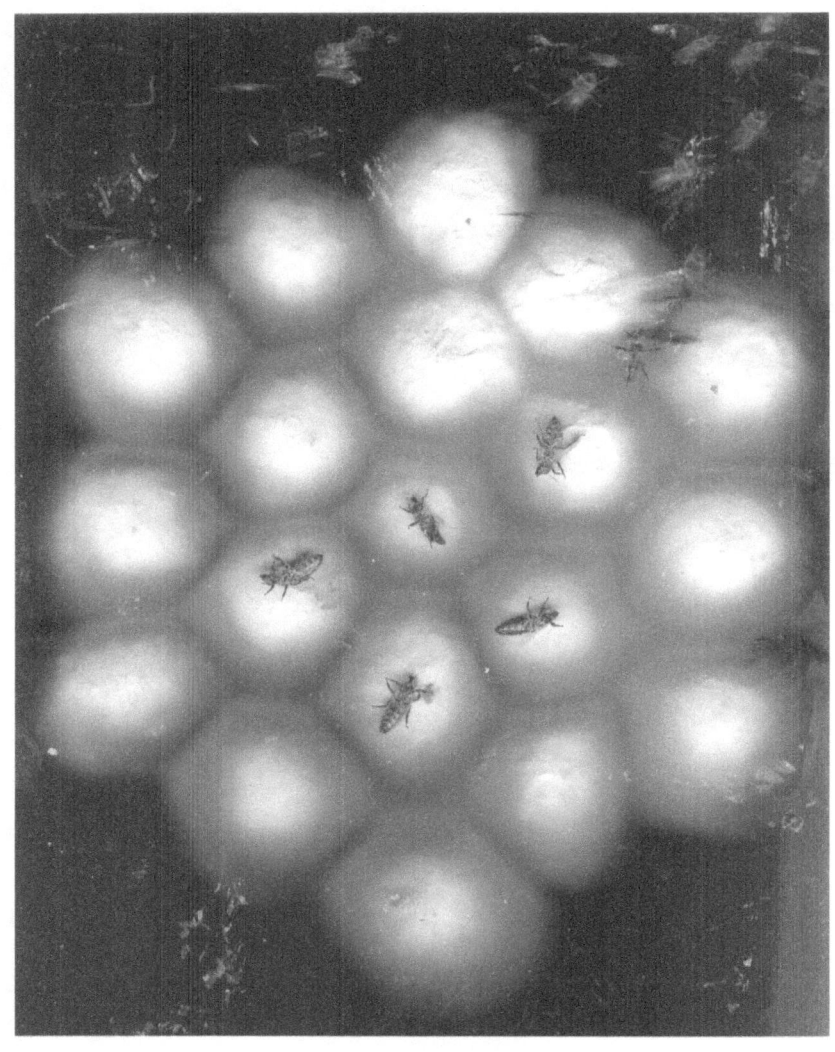

49. *Hive Scan*, 2001-2003
collaboration between Aganetha and Richard Dyck

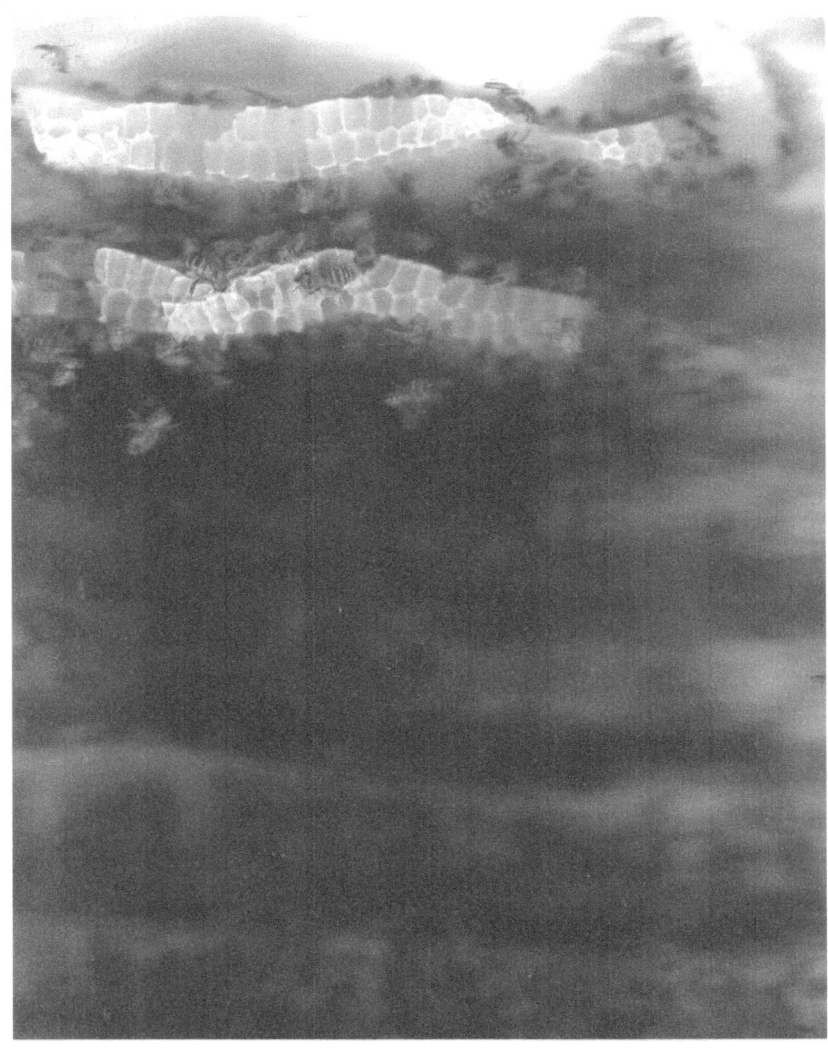

50. *Hive Scan*, 2001-2003
    collaboration between Aganetha and Richard Dyck

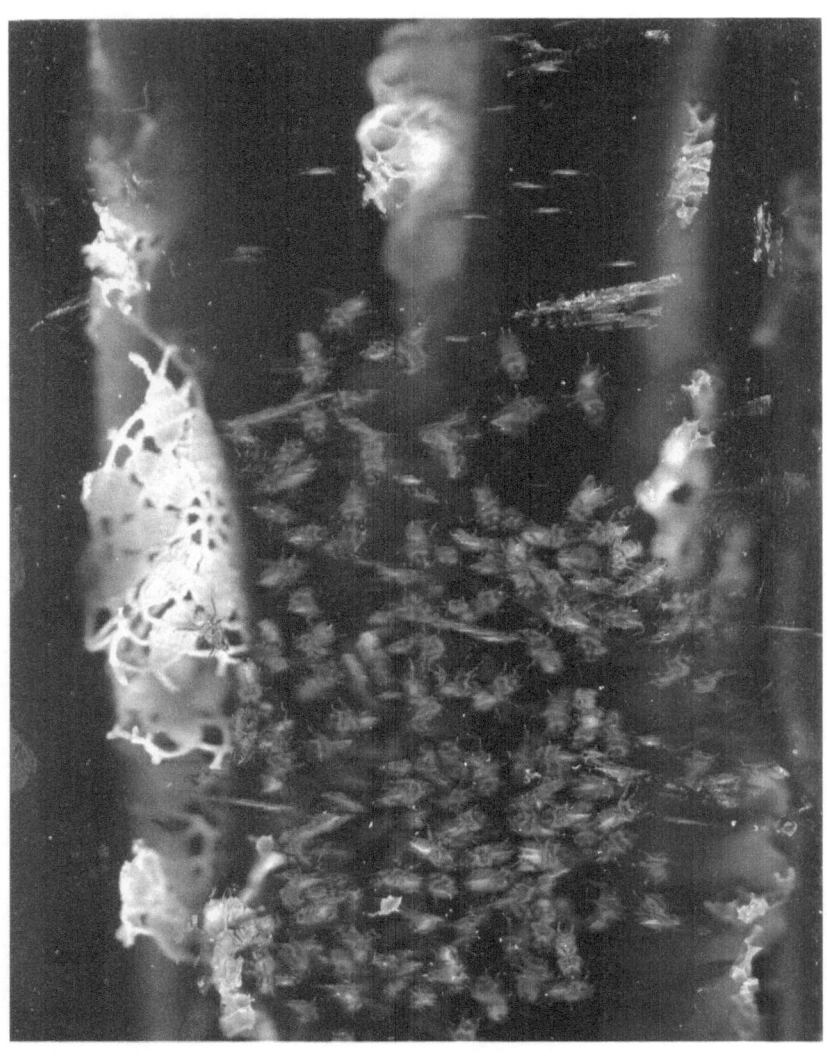

51. *Hive Scan*, 2001-2003
   collaboration between Aganetha and Richard Dyck

scans picturing fragmented instances of light refracted back off still and moving elements within this interiorized environment, the distortions of which bring to mind other-than-human optical modes of perception. There is a balance found in these works that brings human and honeybee perspectives into contact, not directly but rather through the mediation of technology – communication among different specifies is not possible through direct contact. Said differently, the balancing of human and other-than-human perspectives is made possible in *Hive Scans* through the mediating capacities of technology, which extends our ability to perceive the bees by literally distorting our 'normal' modes of perception. Black folds in upon the lightness of the hive fragments, modulated with material and digital detritus floating amongst an openness, an abyss brought to life by reality fragments – we see a doily on the left side of one image – and abstracted bees that are different points of view made simultaneous. The speculative nature of these photographic images, which encourage us to question our specific ways of seeing, invite further queries regarding the ramifications of our mode of existing on the earth and how this existence affects the rest of the planet.

For this reason, works from this series function well within the 2012 traveling exhibition *Nature's Toolbox: Biodiversity, Art, and Invention*, curated by Randy Jayne Rosenberg, an international exploration of art and ecology as a call for change. While not blatantly ecological, specifically in terms of the imagery, it is the wider implication of *Hive Scans* that is discussed in the catalogue accompanying the exhibition.

> The drastic increase in the use of toxic pesticides has also taken their terrible toll on bees. According

to a recent estimate, 95% of the wild bees in North America have died in the last few years due to lowered resistance to mites, and farmed honeybees are being kept alive, as Aganetha puts it, by "all sorts of trial and error and tons of medication" (Dyck 1999). And now there is the new worry that genetically modified crops are killing and/or mutating butterflies and other insects in disastrous numbers. Dyck['s] most recent research asks questions about the human ramifications should honeybees disappear from earth.[46]

But, again, Aganetha and Richard Dyck ask these questions not directly but rather in and through the intermediate processes that embody the ideals of biodiversity. As images of the material and conceptual space between humans and bees, these photographic works ask a question that guides Dyck's approach to the bees: "What ramifications are there to all living beings, should the honeybees disappear from earth?"[47]

It is this form of creative mediation that also drives the series that Aganetha Dyck produced with the photographer William Eakin, under the title *Light*. In these works Dyck continues to aid the bees in producing honeycombed sculptures, with Eakin literally acting as a middleman facilitating Dyck's interactions with her honeybee collaborators – he also supplied the items used. The indirectness of this process is signaled through the pairing of the actual altered objects with photographic representations of these sculptural objects, the photographs reflecting Eakin's own approach to art. In the brochure for the 2016 exhibition *Animal Intent*, curator Emily Falvey notes: "Eakin placed a selection of vintage table lamps from his personal collection in the hives. Dyck participated remotely, giving instructions via a cell phone. Eakin then re-appropriated the completed sculptures in a series of distorted photographs that quietly fold collaboration back into estrangement."[48] Also included in the 2014 exhibition *Toxicity*, this quality of otherworldliness or *estrangement* invites us to re-imagine our perspective on and relationship with the fundamental systems of behaviours and dispositions that determine our understandings of the world. (In the following chapter Miriam and I focus on a detailed examination of this project.)

*

Aganetha Dyck's materialization of interspecies mediation extends her investment in the creativity of the bees, specifically their ability to interact with and alter objects. "For me the give and take with the honeybees and my art practice *includes* communication via materials," she tells me.[49] In her practice honeybees are not just collaborators, they are also a natural technology or, more properly, *techné* that is at once the material being of the bees and the specific modes of their practice.

From her chance encounter with the BEE MAID sign to the elaborate installation of *The Extended Wedding Party* we witness Dyck's participation with the *techné* of the bees, her active engagement with their material and practical modes of being; in *Hive Scans* we see her initiating a mediated form of engagement with the honeybees' practices that invites more extensive considerations of and intercommunications with the bee's *techné*. It is the relational quality of mediation that defines the parameters of her post-bee works, in which the question of interspecies communication, especially between the worlds of bees and humans, is explored using two main creative strategies.

On the one hand Dyck engages with the honeybees from a distance, their collaboration now taking on an active quality of mediation – functioning through another presence. We see this in the use of technology in *Hive Scans* and the photographic works in *Light*. We also witness this in her acceptance of intermediaries in the process of altering objects with the bees, people who have contact with the bees on her behalf; the altered works in this case are accomplished with the help of other people who mediate her relationship with the bees. William Eakin performed this role in their project *Light*.

More recently, Dyck has been commissioned by Robert Blackson at the Tyler School of Art at Temple University in Philadelphia to complete a series of bee works over several seasons. She sent a number of objects to the gallery in 2015, all of which she prepared beforehand with wax in her studio. These were accompanied by instructions on particular placements, as well as addition and subtraction of honeycomb or beeswax – important communications that define her relationship with the bees, which, even at a distance, remains tied to her engagement with the *techné* of their being and practice. These works were displayed in the gallery inside a cabinet, where the honeybees were able to continue working on the objects (again through Plexiglas tubes leading outside the exhibitionary space). In this way, Dyck positions herself as a mediator between the human and the bee elements of the working process.

On the other hand Dyck's overall consideration of mediation allows her to focus more intently on the *habitus* of the bees, specifically through considerations

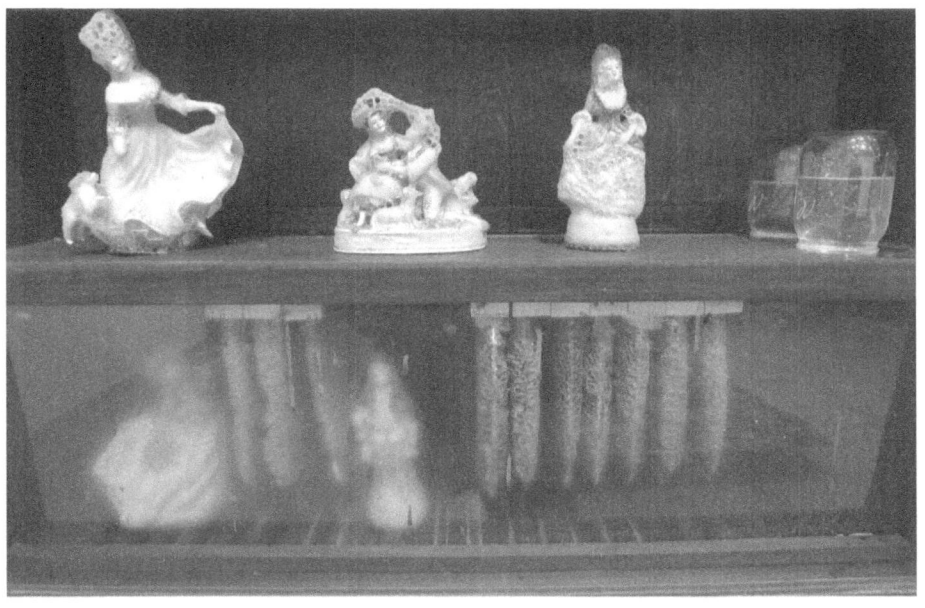

52. *Aganetha Dyck and her Swarm of Bees* [detail], 2016-17
    installation view at Tyler School of Art, Temple University

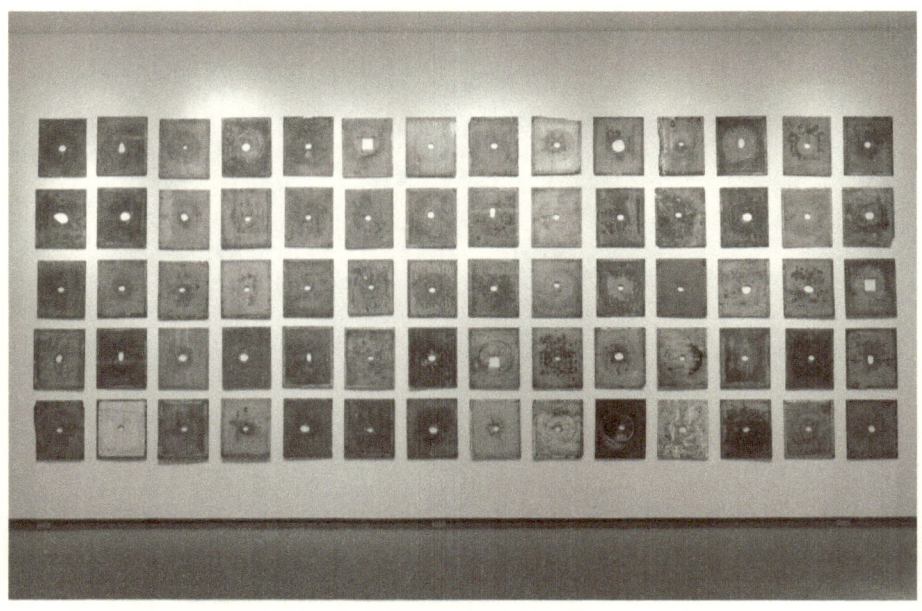

53. *Denouement: Memories of the Hive*, 2015
installation view at Tom Thomson Art Gallery
photograph by Willy Waterton

of the vital material systems of the life of honeybees as moments of communication. Since her first encounter with the bees she has been collecting apiary items and by-products, some of which were used within her works. For example, we can recall the employment of hive boxes to display the altered shoes and to showcase the altered sports equipment in the outdoor installation *Sports Night in Canada,* and the use of hive blankets in creating formal clothing in *The Extended Wedding Party.* In her post-bee works she extends this practice by focusing on the material realities of these items, which are "bee encrusted 'messages'," according to the artist. In my discussion with her she states: "So here I am, thinking of what to do with these materials ... they are beautiful finds. A few of the feeder boards resemble hieroglyphics or codes yet to be cracked. Others leave marks, tracings or prints, of how honeybees create honeycomb. There is much to discover as I clean all these materials."

These works, which Dyck poetically refers to as *hive finds,* present the material traces left behind by the bees in their own (man-made) environments, specifically on the elements that make up the beehive. Her series of apiary feeder boards are particularly impressive. These rectilinear wooden boards are used in times of food and resource shortage to replace the normal cover for the hive, which allows the beekeeper to attach a container of sugar syrup to a hole cut into the middle of the surface that helps the bees work through this period. She collected over 200 of these feeder boards, which appear in various states of coloration and wear, some with additional elements (often metal), each sporting a differently formed hole. The resulting objects are understood and treated by the artist as moments

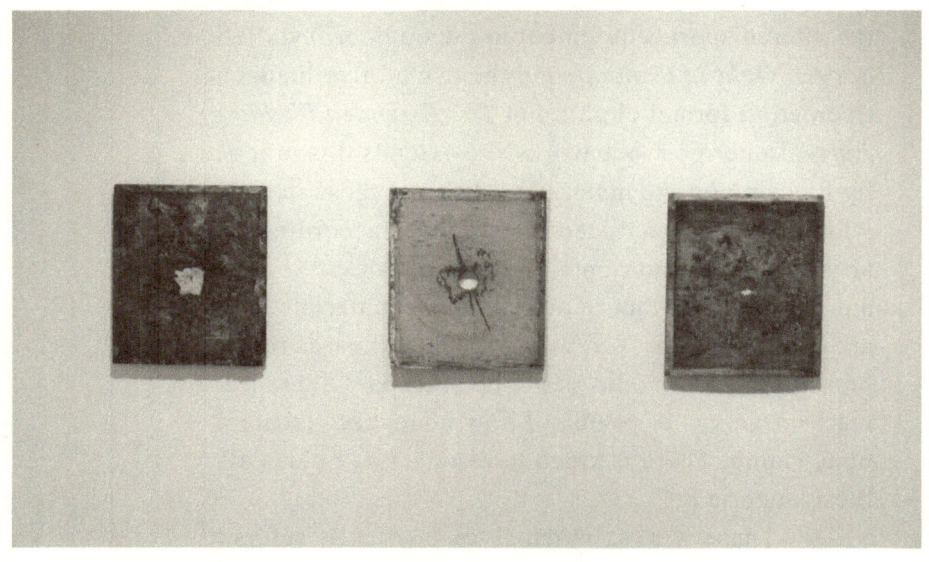

54. *Feeder Boards*, 2016
 installation view at Michael Gibson Gallery
 image courtesy Michael Gibson Gallery

of creative potential, allowing us to witness in the function of their existence a living poetry of the bees materialized on the surface of these boards. For this reason, Dyck gives primary authorship of the objects to the bees, with her taking on the role of creatively *altering* these finds. Given the relative uniformity of their sizes, these boards are presented as a compelling series of works that at once reflects upon and extends the conceptual space of the canvas – as a *window unto another world*, a world that belongs to human and other-than-human beings alike.

When installed in the Tom Thomson Gallery from 2015 to 2016, in a curated exhibition by Virginia Eichhorn, these *Feeder Boards* were arranged on the wall in a grid, five high and fourteen wide. Viewing these works one gets caught up in exploring the various markings found on these repeated surfaces: some bee-made and some human-made (and yet others are animal or insect made). Each board functions as a moment of mediation, spaces through which one can consider the cosmogony of the bees and how we exist in relation to the possibility of this shared world – one that quite intentionally invites contemplation. This is why Dyck wants us to recognize the bees' work as a language, one that can be translated. "I would like people to contemplate the marks that the honeybees left on the feeder boards," which Dyck refers to as "possible messages from the hives."[50]

In a dedicated exhibition of these *Feeder Boards* at the Michael Gibson Gallery in 2016, the works were presented on the walls in a single row, all at the same height, reflecting common hanging practices for canvases in which each work is given its "space." In this arrangement we read the boards as we walk through the

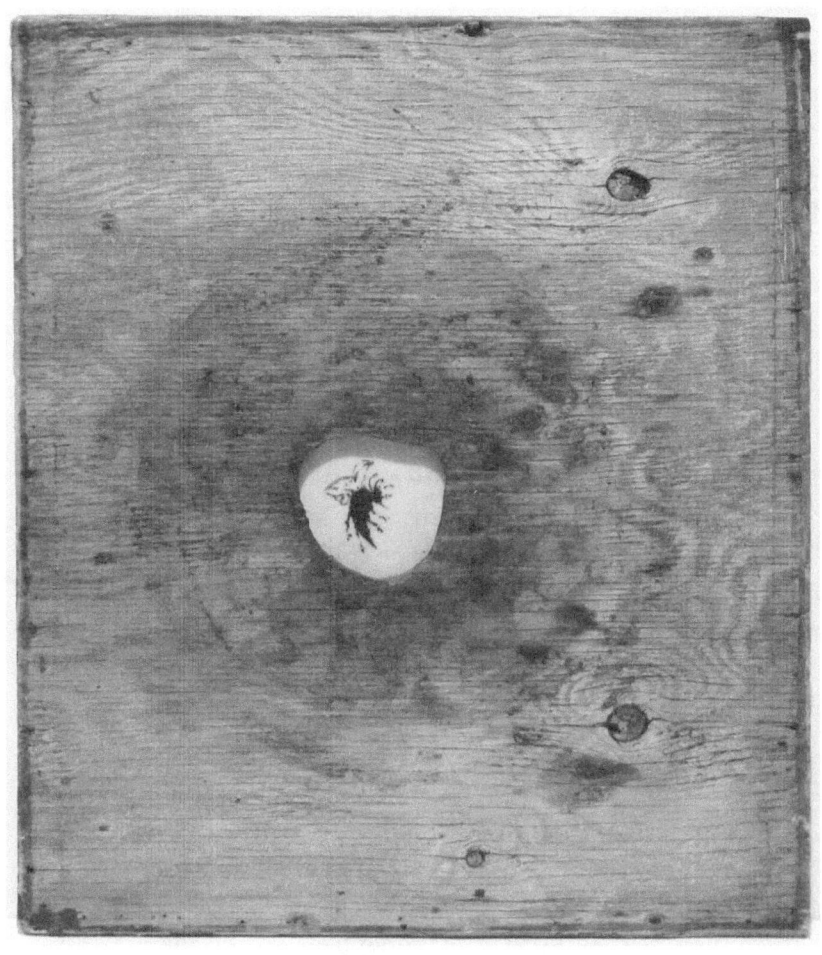

55. *Beekeeper's Red Note*, 2012-16
image courtesy Michael Gibson Gallery

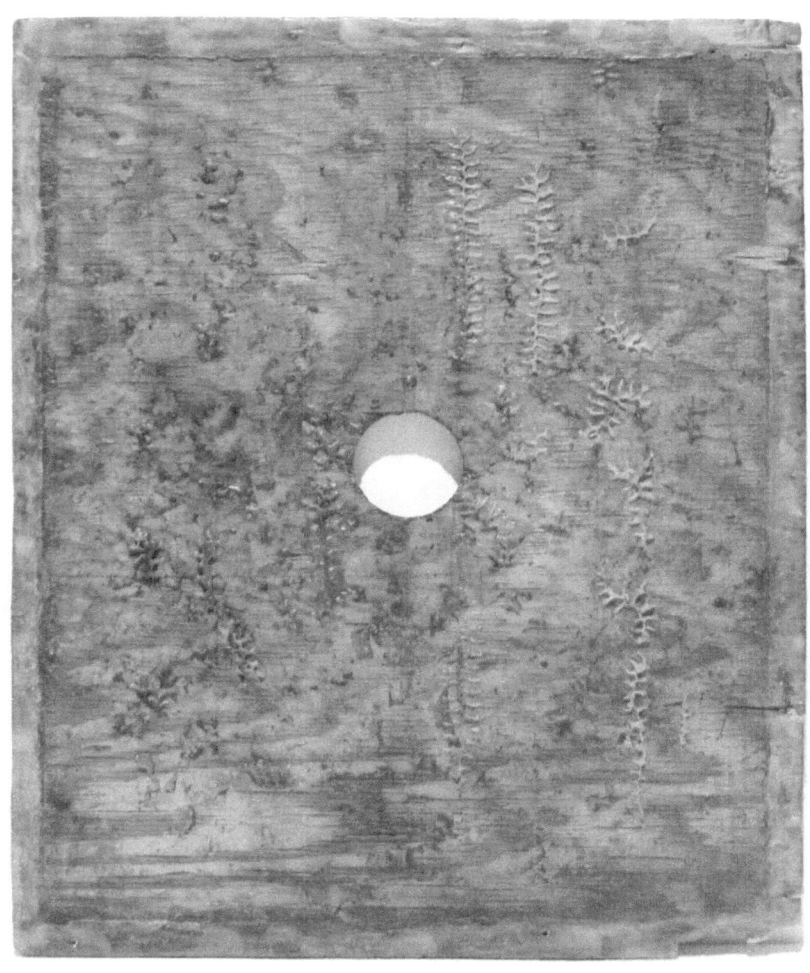

56. *Honeybee's Alphabet*, 2012-16
image courtesy Michael Gibson Gallery

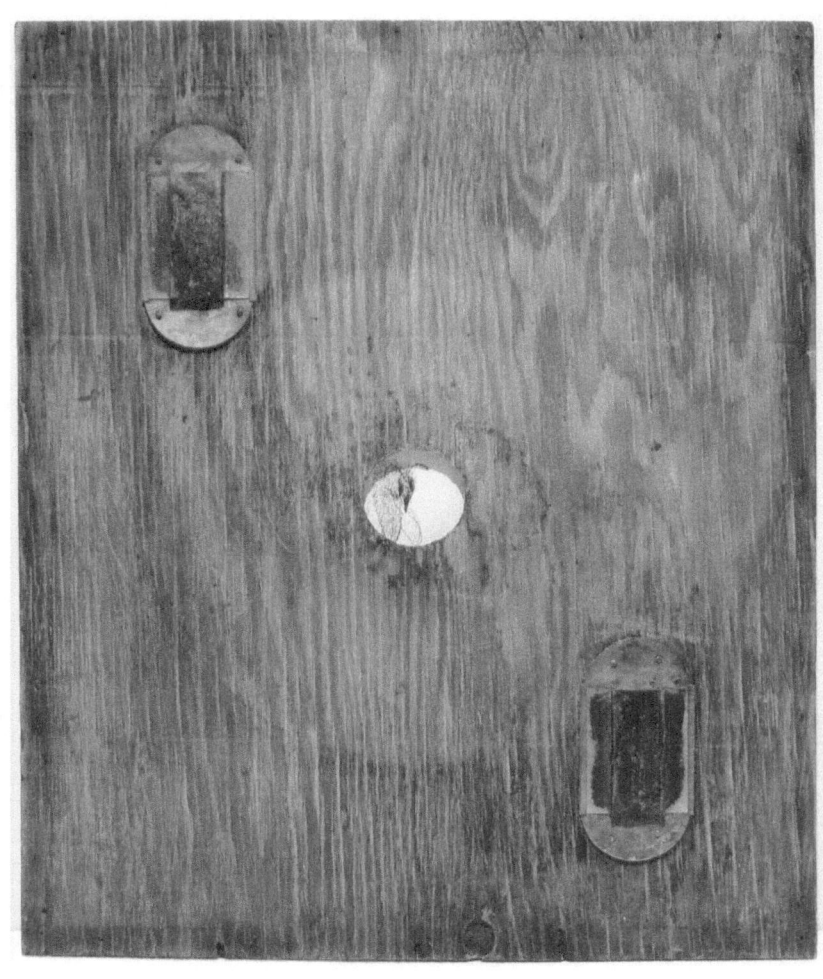

57. *The Escape*, 2012-16
image courtesy Michael Gibson Gallery

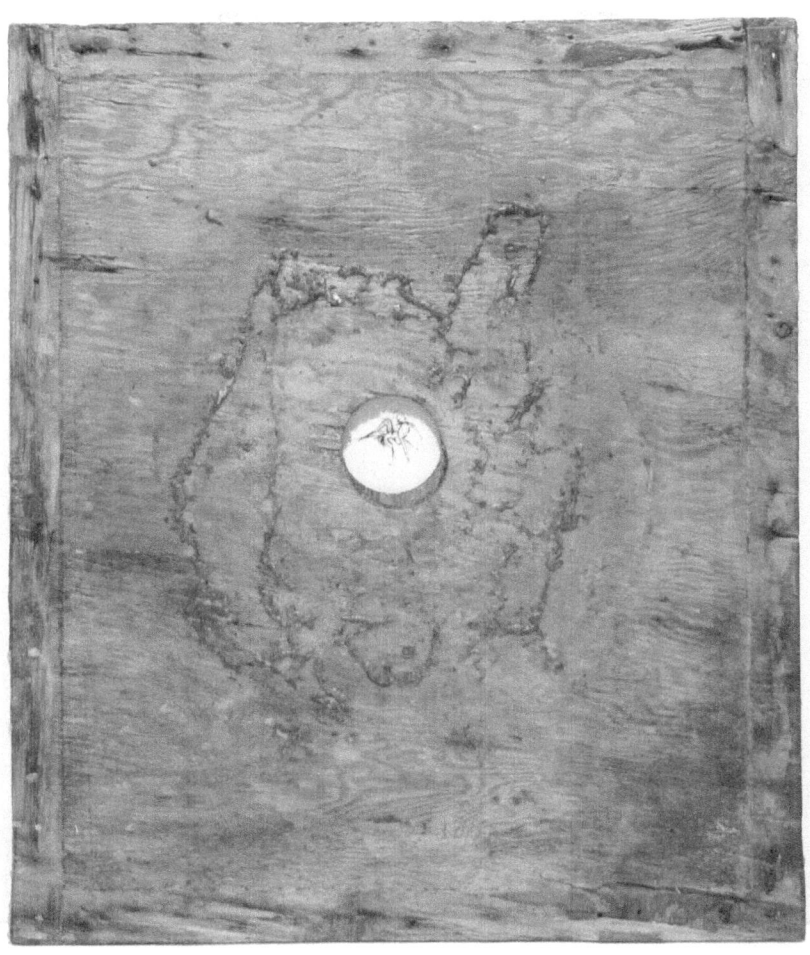

58. *Secret Map of the Drawing Class*, 2012-16
image courtesy Michael Gibson Gallery

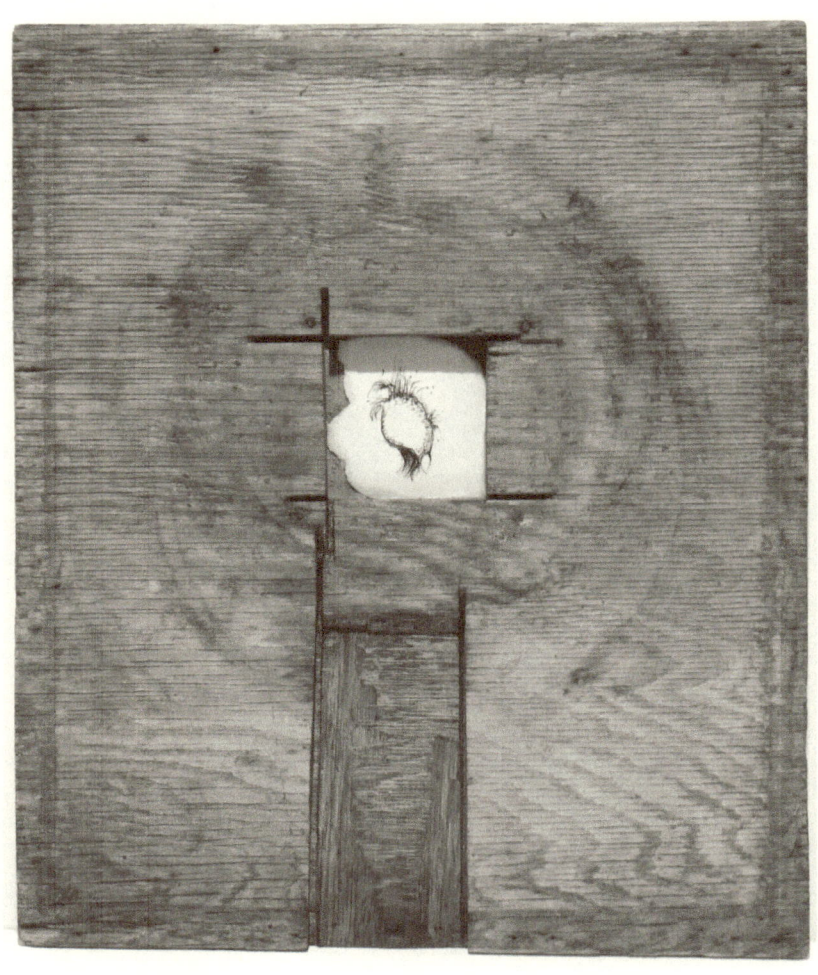

59. *A Message From The Blind Beekeeper*, 2012-16
image courtesy Michael Gibson Gallery

gallery, each being encountered individually as well as part of a sequence of communications. Dyck adds her drawings of bees to these works, which we discover framed by the variously formed holes that define the previous functionality of these boards.

The identity of the works is crucial and plays into the idea of these *Feeder Boards* as captured moments of trans-species dialogues, sometimes literal and other times mysterious or marvellous. This quality is acknowledged by Dyck in her imaginative titles, which include: *Beekeeper's Red Note, Ancient Circle Print, Honeybee Alphabet, The Escape, Tell it to the Bees, Secret Map of the Drawing Class* and (my favourite) *A Message from the Blind Beekeeper*. Here there is a play between reality and imagination that is quite surreal – following the logic of Surrealism as engaging not just with art but rather, more extensively, as a way of engaging with life.[51] And it is in the interplay between bee and human modes of creative communication that Dyck envisions in and on these readymade boards, which she presents as works of art authored by human and other-than-human creators.

*

"Visiting a hive for the first time altered my way of thinking and altered my artistic career."[52] Dyck's words tell us about her being and practice after coming into contact with the bees, who, again, become more then just collaborators in her art but also represent the source for a new way of thinking about and engaging with life. The *hive finds* communicate the elements of this trans-species perception at its most basic, inviting us to question the limits of our experience of the world by showing us a larger reality that is beyond human perceptions and understandings.

This is Dyck's environmentalism, through which she calls attention to threats facing not only the bees but also all life that depends upon these powerful little creatures. It is also, I believe, the foundation for more expansive and inclusive systems of behaviours and meanings that takes into consideration the interrelationship between human and other-than-human beings. Dyck proposes this vision of a global *habitus* by taking seriously the creative nature of honeybees, which she presents through her art as a vital form of knowledge. "It's as if the bees are a thought process," she tells Joan Borsa.[53] And Dyck follows this *thought process* throughout the different and even contradictory ways it develops, creating a collaborative practice that is at one and the same time direct and indirect, physically grounded and emotionally latent.

Notes

1. We were in Winnipeg to present our curated project *The Films and Videos of Jamelie Hassan*, which was screened on September 25 at Platform: Centre for Photographic and Digital Arts. Hassan also gave a lecture the following day at MAWA, the gallery that provided us with our accommodations.
2. Michaëlle Jean was Governor General of Canada from 2005 to 2010.
3. Sigrid Dahle, "Talking with Aganetha Dyck: A Ten Year Conversation," *Aganetha Dyck* (Winnipeg: Winnipeg Art Gallery and St. Norbert Arts & Cultural Centre, 1995), 22.
4. Shirley Madill, "Out of the Home and into the Hive," *Aganetha Dyck* (Winnipeg: Winnipeg Art Gallery and St. Norbert Arts & Cultural Centre, 1995), 8.
5. Aganetha Dyck to Roger Balboni and Sylvie Marandon, "Interview with the Artist," *Aganetha Dyck* (Paris: Services culturels de l'Ambassade du Canada, 2001), 76.
6. Dyck to Balboni and Marandon, "Interview with the Artist," 77.
7. Nancy Tousley, "Aganetha Dyck," *Canadian Art* 9.3 (Fall 1992): 63-64.
8. Elizabeth Legge, private conversation, July 18, 2016. It was important to Legge that "Aganetha told a mutual friend that this was the first work she ever sold." Dyck

had taken a 19th century art history class with Legge, who remembered the artist being especially enthused by Jean-Baptiste Greuze's painting *A Girl with a Dead Canary* (1765), noting that "Aganetha liked playful symbolism."

9. Dahle, "Talking with Aganetha Dyck: A Ten Year Conversation," 18.
10. See Katharine Breen, *Imagining an English Reading Public, 1150-1400* (Cambridge: Cambridge University Press, 2010), 17-18.
11. Pierre Bourdieu, "Postface to Erwin Panofsky, Gothic Architecture and Scholasticism," trans. Laurence Petit, in Bruce Holsinger, in *The Premodern Condition: Medievalism and the Making of Theory* (Chicago: The University of Chicago Press, 2005), 233.
12. Bourdieu, "Postface to Erwin Panofsky, Gothic Architecture and Scholasticism," 226.
13. Dahle, "Talking with Aganetha Dyck: A Ten Year Conversation," 19-20. See also Balboni and Marandon, "Interview with the Artist," 77-78 and Nancy Tousley, "Aganetha Dyck," *Canadian Art* 9.3 (Fall 1992): 63.
14. Nicolas Appert, *The Art Of Preserving All Kinds Of Animal And Vegetable Substances For Several Years* (1811), trans. K. G. Bitting (Chicago: Bacteriologist, Glass Container Association of America, 1920), vii.
15. Aganetha Dyck, quoted in *Aganetha Dyck: Recent Work* (Winnipeg: The Winnipeg Art Gallery, 1984), np.
16. Dyck to Balboni and Marandon, "Interview with the Artist," 78.
17. Dyck to Balboni and Marandon, "Interview with the Artist," 78.
18. Jonathan Bennett's distinction between behaviours that are 'regular' (descriptions of regularities) and

'rule-guided' behaviours support this idea of applying the concept of habitus to other-than-human beings, specifically in his analysis of honeybees. See Jonathan Bennett, *Rationality: An Essay Towards an Analysis* [1964] (Hackett: Indianapolis, 1989).
19. Mason Journal, "Interview with Aganetha Dyck: Canadian Visual Artist," *Mason Journal* (2011): http://www.mason-studio.com/journal.
20. Joan Borsa, "We Have History, They Have Myth," *The Library: Inner/Outer* (Lethbridge: Art Gallery of Southern Alberta, 1991), 15.
21. Borsa, "We Have History, They Have Myth," 15.
22. It should be noted that, as opposed to the other works in the installation, this title does not conform with the one given by the Winnipeg Art Gallery, which has most of these works in its collection. In this case, I decided to use the title as written on the slides given to me by the artist.
23. Mark L. Winston, *The Biology of the Honey Bee* (Cambridge: Harvard University Press, 1991), 1.
24. As a point of interest, the ways in which particular materials are interpreted by the bees was something Dyck had to make herself aware of as she began working with these little beings. Using "fabrics such as velvet, or furs (real or imitation) with the honeybees," for example, "could communicate that perhaps a rat or bear or some foreign creature might be threatening, she tells me. "It would not only be the feel of the fabric, also the scent. If shoes were placed into the hive, they best be new or well cleaned or they were ignored by honeybees." Aganetha Dyck, private conversation, December 31, 2016.
25. Mason Journal, "Interview with Aganetha Dyck," np.
26. Mason Journal, "Interview with Aganetha Dyck," np.

27. Joan Borsa, "The Absent Bride: Intimate Acts & Interior Movements (Aganetha Dyck's Extended Wedding Party)," *Aganetha Dyck* (Winnipeg: Winnipeg Art Gallery and St. Norbert Arts & Cultural Centre, 1995), 56.
28. Borsa, "The Absent Bride," 58.
29. Elizabeth Martin and Vivian Meyer, "Aganetha Dyck," *Female Gazes: Seventy-Five Women Artists* (Toronto: Second Story Press, 1997), 124.
30. Borsa, "The Absent Bride," 56.
31. Juan Antonio Ramirez, *The Beehive Metaphor: From Gaudi to Le Corbusier* (London: Reaktion Books, 2000), 89-90.
32. See Marcel Duchamp, "The Green Box," *The Writings of Marcel Duchamp*, ed. Michel Sanouillet and Elmer Peterson (New York: Da Capo Press, 1973), 26.
33. Aganetha Dyck, quoted in Gilles Hébert, "Aganetha Dyck and the St. Norbert Arts & Cultural Centre," *Aganetha Dyck* (Winnipeg: Winnipeg Art Gallery and St. Norbert Arts & Cultural Centre, 1995), 60.
34. Mark L. Winston, *Bee Time: Lessens from the Hive* (Cambridge: Harvard University Press, 2014), 155.
35. Dyck, quoted in Gilles Hébert, "Aganetha Dyck and the St. Norbert Arts & Cultural Centre," 60.
36. Aganetha Dyck, private correspondence, November 16, 2010.
37. Winston, *Bee Time: Lessons from the Hive*, 155.
38. Mason Journal, "Interview with Aganetha Dyck," np.
39. Dyck to Balboni and Marandon, "Interview with the Artist," 83.
40. Francis Huber, *New Observation Upon Bees* [1814], trans. C. P. Dadant (Hamilton: American Bee Journal, 1926), 5.

41. Di Brandt, "Working in the Dark," *Ecclectica* (the Arts Edition, 2009): http://ecclectica.brandonu.ca/issues/2009/1/. This text is a fragment of her essay "& then everything goes bee: A Poet's Journal," in *So This Is the World & Here I Am in It* (Edmonton: NeWest Press, 2007).
42. Aganetha Dyck, quoted in Brandt, "Working in the Dark," np.
43. Brandt, "Working in the Dark," np.
44. Robin Laurence, "Aganetha Dyck: The Wild Lies All Around Us," *Aganetha Dyck: Collaborations* (Burnaby: Burnaby Art Gallery, 2009), 14.
45. Winston, *The Biology of the Honey Bee*, 129.
46. Randy Jayne Rosenberg, *Nature's Toolbox: Biodiversity, Art, and Invention* (San Francisco: Natural World Museum, 2012), np.
47. Aganetha Dyck, private conversation, December 31, 2016.
48. Emily Falvey, *Animal Intent* (New York: apexart, 2016), np.
49. Aganetha Dyck, private conversation, December 31, 2016.
50. Aganetha Dyck, quoted in Shannon Moore, "A Poignant Farewell: Aganetha Dyck at the Tom Thomson Gallery," *NGC Magazine* (September 28, 2015): http://www.ngcmagazine.ca/correspondents/a-poignant-farewell-aganetha-dyck-at-the-tom-thomson-gallery.
51. Anna Balakian, *Surrealism: The Road to the Absolute* (Chicago: University of Chicago Press, 1987), 49.
52. Aganetha Dyck, private conversation, December 31, 2016.
53. Aganetha Dyck, quoted in Borsa, "The Absent Bride," 50.

Aganetha Dyck and William Eakin's *Light*
by Miriam Jordan-Haladyn and Julian Jason Haladyn

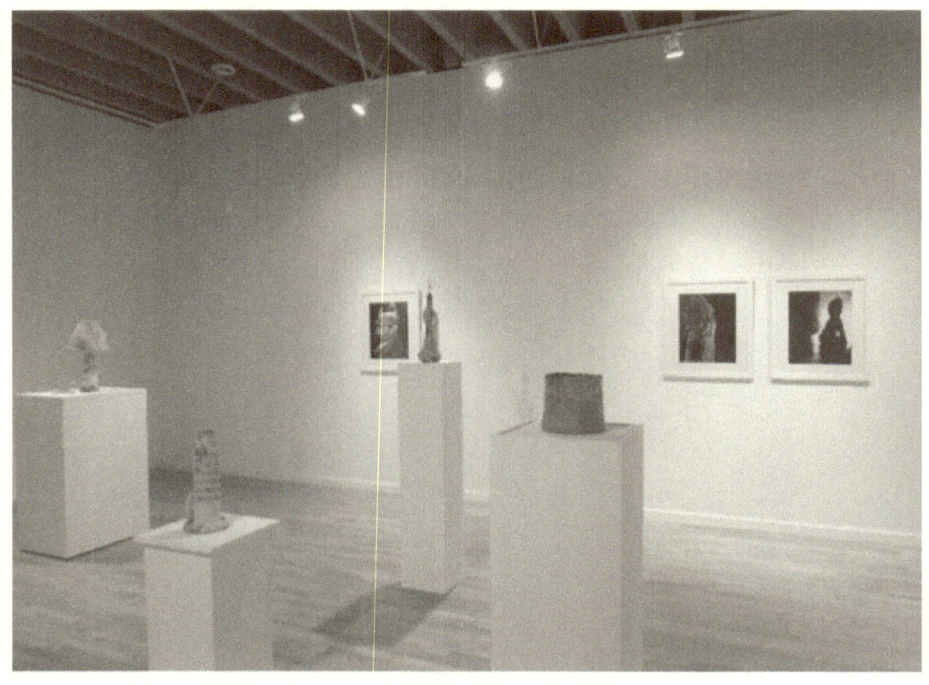

60. *Light*, 2011
 collaboration between Aganetha Dyck and William Eakin
 installation view at Michael Gibson Gallery
 image courtesy Michael Gibson Gallery

For the exhibition *Light*, presented at the Michael Gibson Gallery, Aganetha Dyck and William Eakin bring together their unique approaches to art in a dynamic collaboration. In their individual practices, both artists have continuously transformed found objects through subtle processes of alteration, revealing the minute beauty and material qualities of ordinary objects. Dyck is well known for her twenty-year partnership with honeybees that has grown out of her interest in their construction of space through the production of beeswax and honey, which they make from the crop of nectar and pollen collected while pollinating plants. Dyck is keenly interested in the crucial role that bees play in the ecosystem; without bees the pollination of food crops is jeopardized. She has collaborated extensively with these communal insects by placing a variety of reclaimed objects into their hives, allowing the bees to alter the forms and images by covering them with delicate networks of honeycombs.

  Eakin has a similar fascination with found objects, which he carefully organizes into collections and transforms from the mundane to the extraordinary through his sensually lush approach to photography. His photographs are well known for their uncanny ability to reframe ordinary objects as profound commentaries on the human psyche, reflecting, for instance, the creative impulse to amass collections of ordinary things and how belongings accumulate both meaning and value. In Dyck and Eakin's new collaboration, *Light*, they present an engaging sculptural and photographic project that brings their separate practices into a collaborative dialogue: table lamps assembled by Eakin are transformed in collaboration with Dyck and the bees into sculptures that are in turn photographed by Eakin.

*

Over the last two years, since being diagnosed with a severe allergy to bee stings, Dyck has had to reposition her work with honeybees, a collaboration that has come to define her artistic practice. Prior to the development of her allergy, she engaged directly with the bees by placing objects in the hives and moving them to orchestrate the laboring bees. For the work presented in *Light*, Dyck took on a supervisory role and interacted from a distance with her miniature partners, directing Eakin via cell phone as he worked in the apiary.

The lamps used in this series of works where chosen by Eakin from his extensive collection of collections. In Eakin's solo projects, he gathers and arranges objects – such as tattered found photographs in *Fading Dream* (2009), cookie tins in *Night Garden* (2000) and trophies in *Monument* (1994) – in enlivening configurations before photographing them. With the lamp collection, there is a shared functionality that connects otherwise visibly disparate items. The lamps themselves are unique in their charming quirkiness; among them is a wooden Mickey Mouse, a baroque couple lavishly rendered in ceramic, a matador swirling his red cape

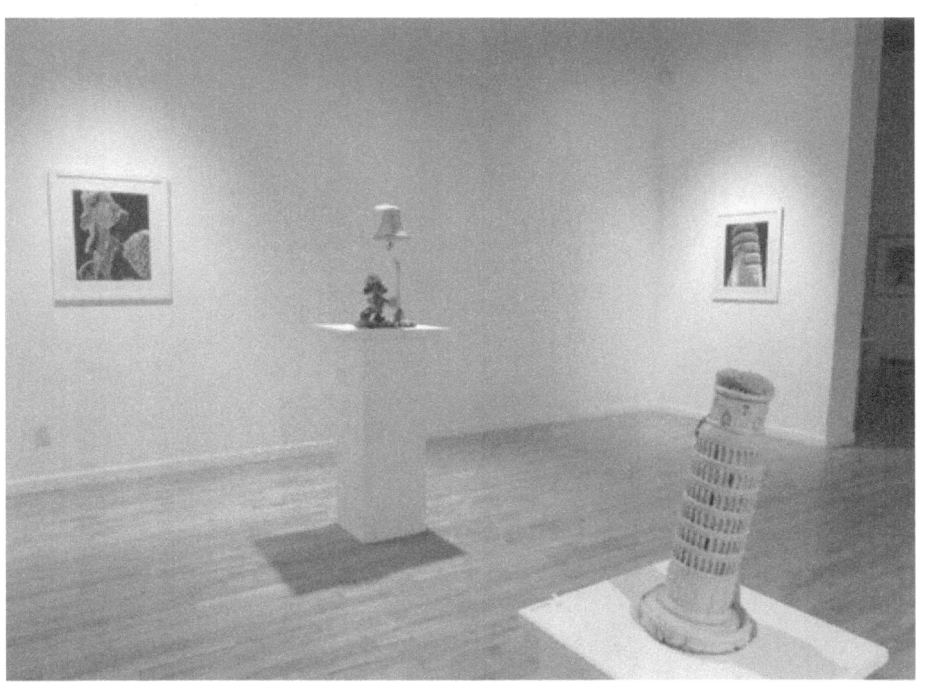

61. *Light*, 2011
   collaboration between Aganetha Dyck and William Eakin
   installation view at Michael Gibson Gallery
   image courtesy Michael Gibson Gallery

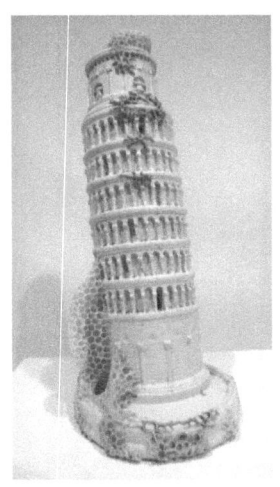

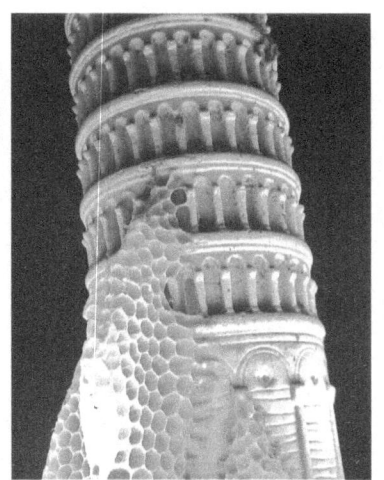

62. *Leaning Tower of Pisa*, 2011
    Aganetha Dyck
    image courtesy Michael Gibson Gallery

63. *Light 0009*, 2011
    William Eakin

behind him, a green giant foot with elves sitting on it, a cartoonish squirrel, a souvenir leaning tower of Pisa and a clear green glass arm with a hand holding a downward facing dagger. The lamps are the scale of bedside table lamps and possess a fantastical dream-like quality, which Eakin emphasizes with his dramatic photographs.

Once the bees completed their work on the seven lamps, Eakin photographed them in his studio with a toy camera. As a result of the deliberately distorting lens of the camera, the lamps seem to glow against dark backdrops with a hyperreal gleam that is almost hallucinogenic in its clarity. Seen with the physical lamps, these photographic worlds heighten the already intense play of object and image. The soft yellow beeswax creates meandering hexagonal patterns across the surfaces of the lamps and emits a delicate scent into the space of the gallery, further heightening the sensorial quality of Eakin's photographs.

There is an interesting back and forth visual exchange among the various pieces on display, with the photographs of the beeswax-encrusted lamps revealing surface features and glowing colours that are not immediately obvious in the sculptures themselves, which are arrayed in front of or near the photographs. What is most striking about the relationship between Dyck and Eakin's works is the material presence the project as a whole offers, with the lamps giving a kind of "reality" to the photographs, which themselves reveal the underlying miniature worlds of the honeycomb covered lamps. Dyck's sculpture *Leaning Tower of Pisa* (2011) is covered with a lacy web of honeycombs that seem to be growing right out of the miniature arches of the tower. Eakin's photograph of the same sculpture *Light 0009* (2011) spectacularly enlarges the diminutive lamp to

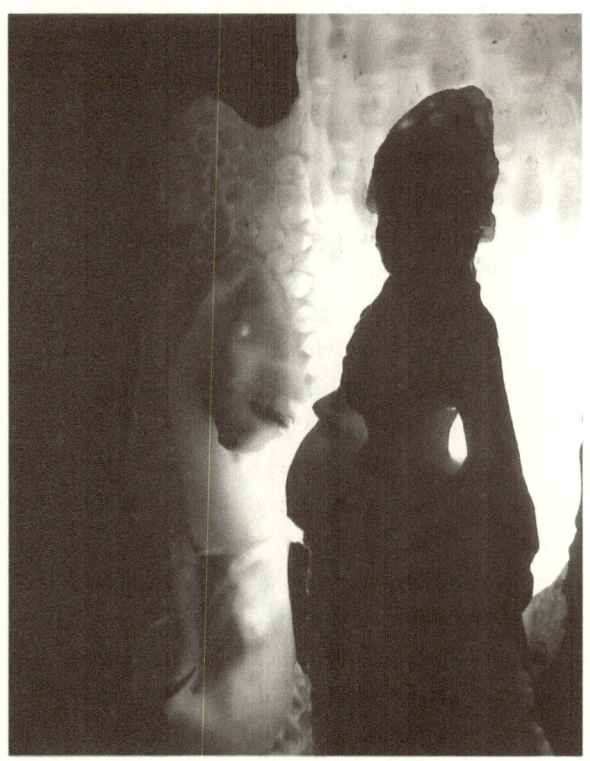

64. *Light 0007*, 2011
    William Eakin

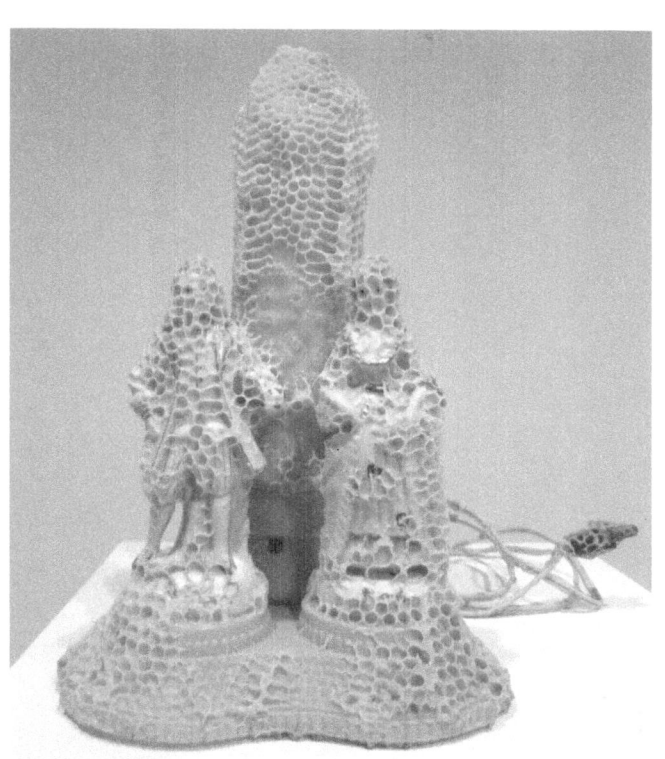

65. *Pink Pillar with Couple*, 2011
    Aganetha Dyck
    image courtesy Michael Gibson Gallery

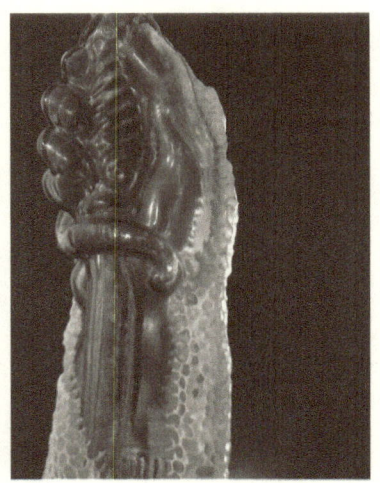

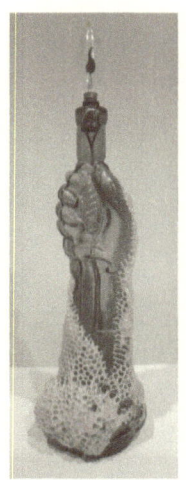

66. *Light 0073*, 2011
    William Eakin

67. *Green Hand*, 2011
    Aganetha Dyck
    image courtesy Michael Gibson Gallery

larger-than-life, emphasizing the monumental nature of the organically fused tower and honeycombs through a dramatic play of light and shadows.

In *Light 0007* (2011) he backlights Dyck's *Pink Pillar with Couple* (2011), creating a surreal shadow of the female figure's beehive hairdo in front of a honey-coloured mesh of wax cells, which fade into purple and then darkness. The altered lamp itself reflects the passage of time through the wax traces left behind by the bees, which obscure the features of the elaborately dressed couple and render them ghostly specters.

Though Dyck and Eakin both present us with the same objects, they are radically different in their sculptural and photographic formats. This juxtaposition emphasizes elements that appear small and inconsequential at first glance, but are profoundly affecting at second glance. Such is the case with Eakin's *Light 0073* (2011), which reveals a translucent green hand emerging from amber beeswax, against a fluctuating violet-black backdrop the lamp glows with an electric luminosity. This prompts a closer look at Dyck's corresponding piece *Green Hand* (2011), which is draped with honeycombs that resonate with an apian energy that eclipses the kitschy qualities of the lamp, transforming it into an oddly alluring sculpture.

Their collaboration is evocative and thoughtfully examines the quiet succession of time and change on these seemingly randomly selected lamps, which were likely cherished by some and disdained by others who previously possessed them. In fact, a similar aesthetic moment occurred between the artists, since Dyck, as she laughingly told us, found several of the lamps to be hideous before the bees changed them.

Conversation with Aganetha Dyck
by Julian Jason Haladyn

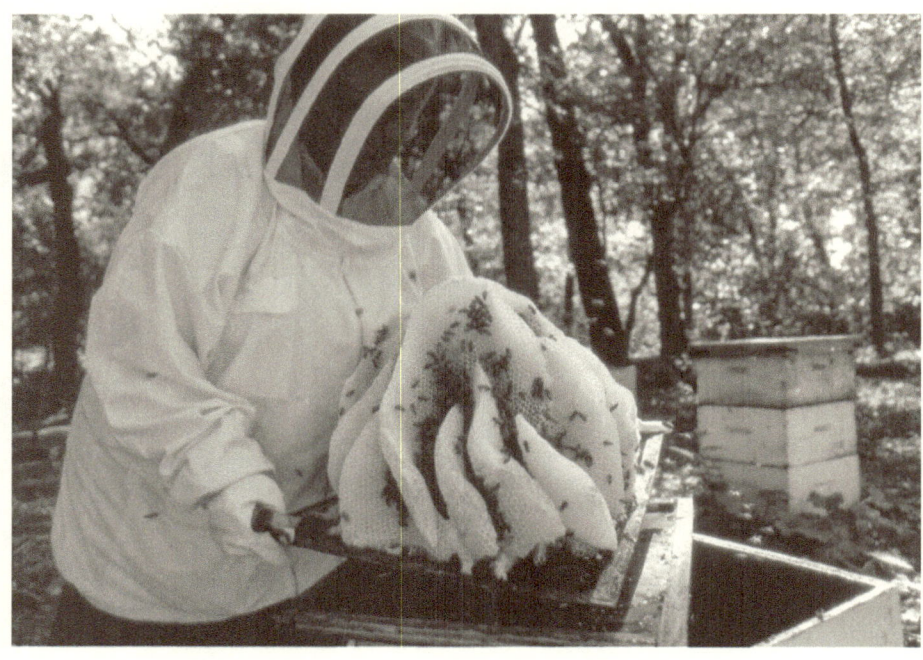

68. Dyck removing *Lost Sculpture* from beehive, 1995
St. Norbert Arts and Cultural Centre Apiary
photograph by William Eakin

1. The Bees

Haladyn—I was hoping you could begin by talking a bit about the bees and how you have come to understand them?

Dyck—I am interested in honeybees and their lives, their many methods of being. I love their warmth, their scent, their tenacity, their movements, their dances, their ways of communicating. They have their own pheromones of communication – chemicals they use to communicate with each other, perhaps with other insects, animals, perhaps with the very flowers they pollinate. Perhaps they are communicating with the very environment we all live in and perhaps they try to communicate with us humans who seldom stop to listen. There are at least 20,000 bee species in the world. My research has led me to visit bee labs, apiaries and beekeepers in Canada, The Netherlands, France and Britain, U.S.A. and Canada.

In the Netherlands I travelled widely visiting apiaries, flower markets, flower auction houses, bee keeping cooperatives, acres of glass houses – literally miles and miles of greenhouses called The Glass City where honeybees pollinated vegetables and flowers. I was informed that the glass city's environment was totally controlled by computers and human caretakers who walked on wooden stilts to reach the high plant filled structures. I visited bee cooperatives for supplies and worked for two months, using wax and honey as materials in a studio at Kunst and Complex, Rotterdam.

In Britain I worked at Yorkshire Sculpture Park with two local beekeepers who collected feral honeybee colonies. I was given a studio for a two-month period and freedom to create and to explore and work with these beekeepers. I learned to hive a wild swarm of honeybees, was given equipment that allowed me to create my own honeybee patterned wax sheeting. Gave talks, worked with adults and children, gave tours of the apiary to art history students from Leeds University. Had an exhibition in the Camellia House, which was built around 1860.

In France I was given a three-month studio at Passages Centre d'Art Contemporain in Troyes, France; I visited an apiary, received the loan of seven ancient beehives from a collector of hives who lived in Paris. Worked and travelled to anything 'honeybee'. Visited wineries and learned the importance of honeybee pollination in the vineyards, and other crops in the area. I gave lectures to the nearby School of Design and a public lecture during my exhibition in Troyes. Had an exhibition at the Canadian Embassy gallery in Paris.

Haladyn—I would love to hear some of the things you admire about the bees.

Dyck—I think of a working beehive as a dark, well-organized place filled with warm, fuzzy, intelligent living beings. I love opening a hive and seeing a carpet of vibrant, brown, living beings dancing the

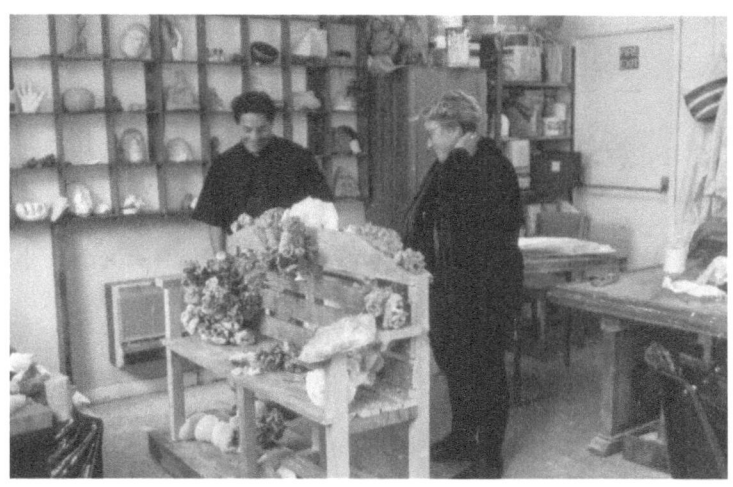

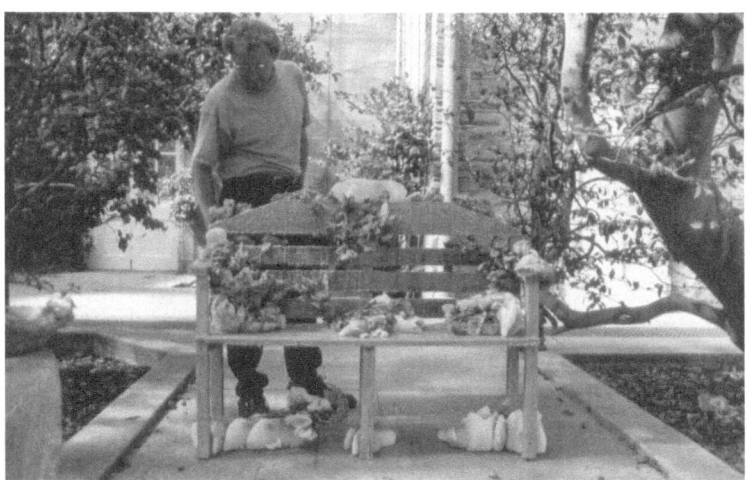

69. Aganetha and Michael Regan with *Park Bench* [in process], 1997
    in Dyck's Yorkshire Sculpture Park studio

70. Honeybees working on *Park Bench*, 1997
    installed in Camellia House
    photographs by Peter Dyck

waggle dance – telling where nectar is abundant. I love hearing the honeybees' thousands of wings buzzing, music sweet to the ears. Listening to the various sounds of communication used by the honeybees is fascinating. I have heard the piping of the Queen Bee prior to her mating flight. The beating of wings is the honeybee's method of controlling the temperature within the hive; it keeps drafts from reaching the Queen as she lays her 1500 to 2000 eggs per day. The beating wings keep the draft from reaching the bee larvae as it nests in its wax cell, waiting to emerge. A new honeybee is anxious to become the hive's new nurse and in a few days she will graduate to become a forager or a guard at the entrance to the hive. She only lives for three to six weeks, her life expectancy depends on the season and her own workload.

 I am fascinated with discovering the various occupants in the hive. The large Queen with her attendants who feed and guide her to the next empty cell, who encourage her to keep laying, who feed her royal jelly, give her water, cleanse her body and murmur softly to her that she is indeed doing just fine, and whispering to her to keep on laying those wee eggs! A Queen Bee mates with a drone bee as she flies approximately 50 feet above the ground – encouraging at least 16 eager drones – the male bees, to mate with her. A successful mating results in enough sperm to keep the Queen laying eggs for three to four years. Mating with a number of drones keeps the bee gene pool healthy and strong.

 Unfortunately, upon mating, the drone bee leaves his entire genitalia embedded within the Queen Bee's body, the drone breaking literally in half, and dying as he hits the ground.

Honeybees are most important for all of earth's living beings, for the earth's eco-system, for crops that feed both humans and animals. Honeybees give us honey, wax, propolis, and pollen. Beeswax is used in the manufacture of cosmetics, car polishing wax, furniture polish, sealing wax, encaustic painting and candle making – to name only a few uses.

I also think of a hive filled with honeybees as unfathomably dark to keep a hive healthy and working, as it must. The hive does not have a place or the space for sick bees, for old bees who cannot keep up with the tasks at hand. Old and infirm honeybees are evicted from the hive and drone bees are evicted near the end of the honey flow season when a well-fertilized Queen Bee no longer requires their services. These 'useless' honeybees are dragged and pushed out of the hive and if they try to return, a group of guard bees will push them still further into the bee yard until they die.

Balling an old Queen Bee can occur when a new Queen has emerged to take over her royal duties. This is something I have only observed via film. Balling the Queen means that a group of bees tightly surround the Queen and, with the heat of their bodies and the use of moisture, they literally boil her to death. There is seldom room for two Queens in a bee colony. Honeybees can ball any foreign creature that enters their hive. However, the bees can also coat the intruder with propolis that embalms it, similar to an insect embalmed in amber. Propolis is a preservative and may keep the insect intact. The temperature of a beehive is kept at 95° Fahrenheit by thousands of honeybees who fan the air within the hive, keeping the temperature steady, not unlike a regular thermostat set at 95° Fahrenheit.

I was ecstatic when a beekeeper pointed to a honeybee excreting wax droplets from her abdomen, this wax material kept building up to eventually become a six sided honeycomb cell. Drone cells require more wax than cells for honey or larvae. Queen Bee cells are the shape of a sewing thimble and are gorgeous structures. I have observed a Queen Bee emerge from her 'thimble of tiny wax cells' and felt like the world was going to be just fine. A colony of honeybees emits sounds of jubilation and also of anticipation when a new Queen emerges.

If an old Queen is still in the hive, the new Queen will threaten her and try to evict her from the hive. If the old Queen resists this threat, the two Queens fight for supremacy until one of them dies. The vigorous new Queen usually wins the battle. The dead Queen is quickly dragged out of the hive by the worker bees. In two days the new Queen will mate with drones and begin laying her 1500 to 2000 eggs per day.

Propolis is a fascinating material. It is the glue the honeybees gather from the tips of evergreens or willow branches and is used to keep bee hives draft free. The worker bees glue the hive boxes and openings of a hive shut with propolis. This means that every time a beekeeper opens and shuts a hive during inspection or honey gathering, the worker bees have to glue the hive back together again.

Haladyn—That is amazing. Thanks to you and your work I have found myself getting very interested in bees. Even before this, I have been aware of the serious threat to bee populations around the world. You must be concerned with the problems facing bees.

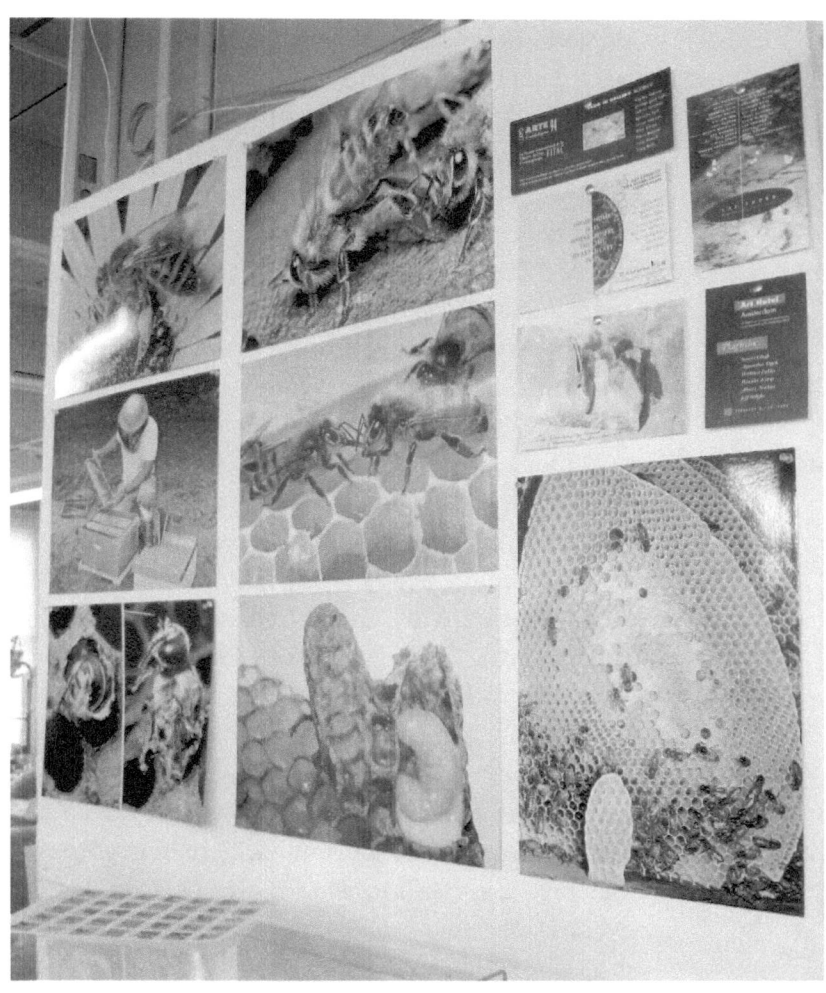

71. View of bee research in Dyck's studio, 2010

Dyck—I am invested in the future of the honeybees and the threat of honeybee extinction. Colony collapse disorder (CCD) is a term used to describe a colony of bees who disappear without a trace and for no obvious reason. CCD has been reported for over one hundred years, however not as frequently and not with the same degree of devastation as it occurs today. Researchers have cited the following as possible causes of recent CCD occurrences: climate change, wars, deforestation, malnutrition, human carelessness or apiary mismanagement, migratory beekeeping, varroa mites, habitat loss, genetics, diseases, and neonicotinoids – pesticides used by chemical companies during crop production. These chemicals are suspected to affect dust, pollen, nectar and the very lives of honeybees. These pesticides are thought to leach into waterways and into the very soil where crops are grown. Companies using neonicotinoid to glue onto crop seeds, claim that the chemical remains on the seeds and is not air borne, therefore does not affect honeybees or other living beings. The media has reported that internet use and airwaves necessary for cell phone use might be causing CCD in honeybees.

The jury is still out in what causes CCD in honeybees.

Haladyn—Your knowledge about the bees continually amazes me. Are there specific people who helped you with your work?

Dyck—There are a number of individuals who have been invaluable to my research and my artistic career.
Dr. Mark L. Winston, Simon Fraser University in Burnaby, B.C., world-renowned bee expert,

recently retired from his bee lab. I spent a week in Dr. Winston's bee lab, following his students during their rounds: a fabulous, unforgettable experience. I learned how to use powerful microscopes. I observed students while they dissected honeybees – during and afterwards, I drew the honeybee's many parts.

Weighing honeybees was fascinating! I was invited to attend a meeting with Dr. Winston, his students and two psychologists who were interested in honeybee behaviour. I observed the honeybees as they performed their waggle dance that informed them that food was within 100 feet of the apiary. I learned that the honeybees use pheromones – chemicals of communication. I learned how to safely melt beeswax and how it adheres to various materials, from Heather Higo, Dr. Winston's assistant. I also learned the properties of beeswax, why it can explode when overheated, why the wax has various scents and colours, that beeswax is snow white until the honeybees walk all over it with pollen and other materials they come in contact with. And I observed Queen cell construction by honeybee workers.

Dr. Stephen Pernal, bee expert at Beaverlodge Bee Lab in Beaverlodge, Alberta, generously shared his knowledge of bee diseases. Hive construction and honeybee adaption to same. At the Beaverlodge Bee Lab I observed Dr. Maria Spivak (who lives in the U.S.A.) artificially inseminate honeybee Queens. Dr. Spivak is a world-renowned specialist in honeybees, especially interested in raising hygienic bees who would keep their hives even more pristine, hopefully learning to rid their hives of mites and diseases without human intervention.

Dr. Otis, now retired, looked after the honeybees in my exhibition at the MacDonald Stewart Art Centre. During this exhibition he invited me to visit his bee lab at the University of Guelph. Dr. Otis's lab housed hundreds if not thousands of bee specimens pinned to a board in a cabinet of drawers. Drawer after drawer of bees, a few as tiny as the head of a pin, others almost as large as the small finger of my hand; blue, green, red, black, orange and multi coloured bees. An amazing sight and a treasure to think about. Not all these bees were honeybees, some were solitary bees, others mason bees, carpenter bees, etc.

I would like to add that my partner Peter Dyck has been unwavering in being there for me over the years. He has been my full-time assistant since he retired in 1996. Even when he was traveling the world as a CESO volunteer, whenever he was home he would construct special hives, shop for materials, invent supports for my sculptures and dress for the bee yard, ready to do whatever was necessary. Without complaining, might I add!

I have also been most fortunate in having an artist son, Richard Dyck, who has collaborated with me on several projects including *The Wax Museum* – also with William Eakin, with the help of a Canada Council Grant. We also collaborated on *Inter Species Communication Attempt* that led to *Hive Scans*, a collaborative project that Richard and I completed in 2000 to 2002 – we can never decide what years we began and exactly when we completed the series of 17 scans, which were edited down from a few hundred scans. I consider the scans as mainly Richard's idea because, as an artist, he was scanning full time when I requested he scan the honeybees as they worked

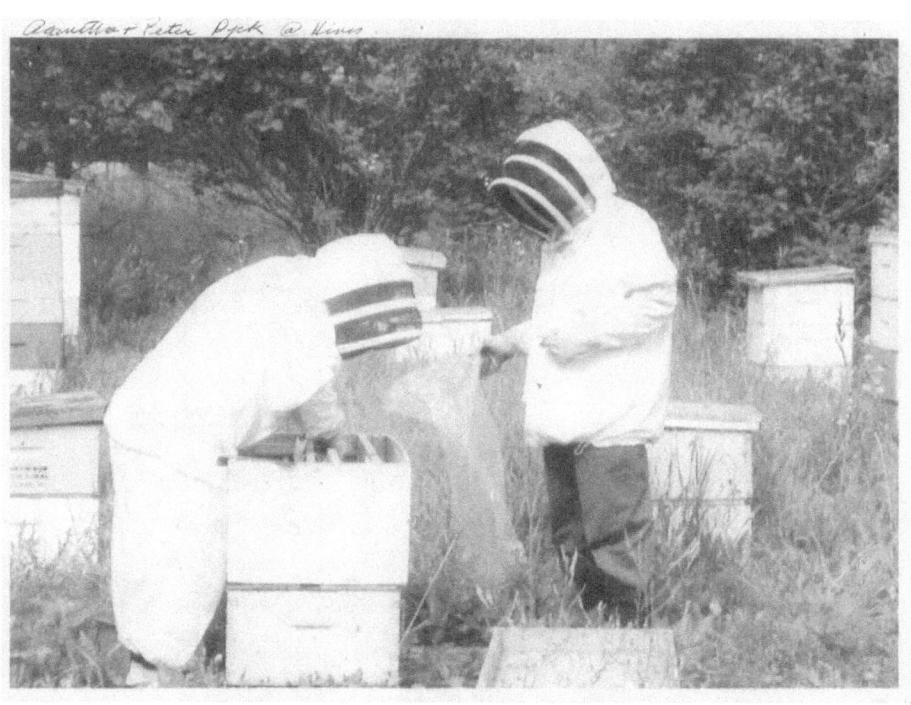

72. Photograph of Aganetha and Peter Dyck at the beehives

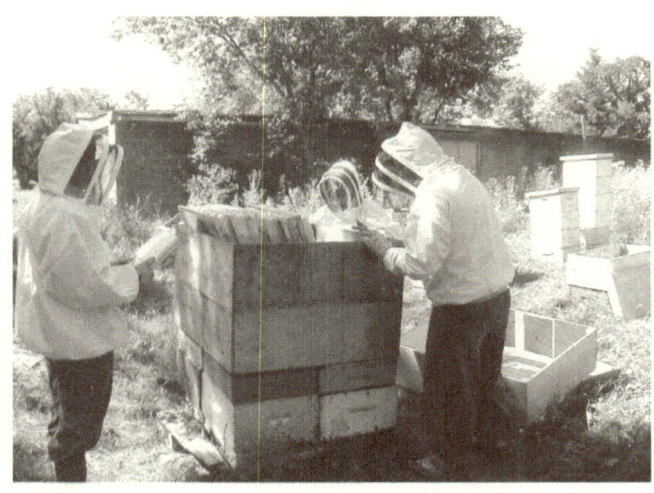

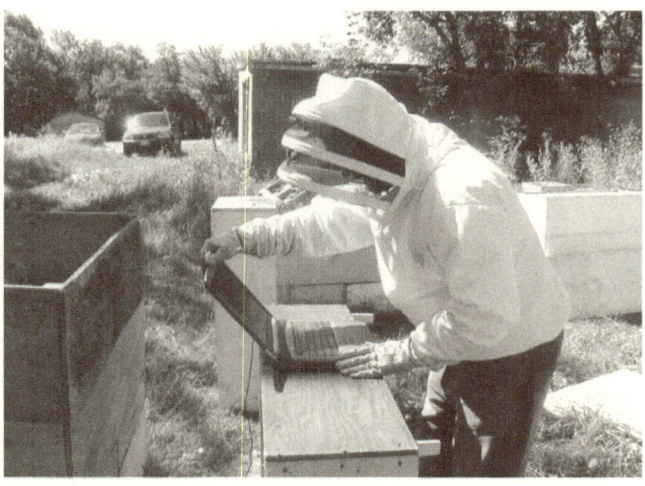

73-74. Aganetha and Richard Dyck working on *Hive Scans*, 2001-2003
photographs by Peter Dyck

on objects that I placed within the darkness of the beehives. Richard took his scanner and computer to the hives, set everything up and my job was to place the scanner into the hives as he operated the computer amidst the apiary. We shared ideas back and forth, it was an amazing adventure. It was a very hot and tiring project – fortunately it ended as a most successful body of work that is in international collections, including the National Gallery of Canada and the Canadian Embassy in Berlin.

My family are all very important to my history, invaluable is what they still are. Michael, a computer-programming architect, and Diane along with Richard and his partner Tricia, manager of Winnipeg's public art program, have been invaluable with internet findings on honeybees, sending me sites and information over the years. Deborah, a high school teacher, is my web master and support guide in many ways. All three of our children's jobs are computer related – so anytime I have an issue with the computer, there are three willing people to call. And yes, when I 'just do not get it computer wise' they do stare at me in disbelief.

Haladyn—Have you found your engagement with the scientific and historical aspect of the bees an important part of producing your artworks with them? In a sense, do you see this history in your work?

Dyck—I definitely see this history in my work. I have found my engagement with the honeybees, the scientific community most important – my artwork took many interesting turns after meeting Mark L. Winston, his assistant Heather Higo and students at Simon Fraser University. Although I did not understand everything, I learned so very much. One week in a lab is simply a wee taste of what the lab has to offer. The students asked if I was taking notes and keeping track of any findings – and no, I was not taking 'scientific' type notes. I was simply an observer, a sponge amidst incredible work being undertaken in the bee lab.

Every lab, every apiary held surprises; scientists, beekeepers are amazing inventors out of curiosity and necessity. Unless a beekeeper has an unusually strong honey yield with over 1000 or more hives, it is unfathomable how the beekeeper can make a living. Beekeeping is not unlike other farming practices, much depends on the weather, crops and health of animals. And a scientist depends on funding support of another kind to feed the research so important to humanity.

As an example, Phil Veldhuis, the beekeeper who has assisted me for approximately 20 years, lost over half his honeybees this spring. Phil had 1,200 strong hives in 2012. This year he has only 600 weak to strong hives – most of them are new starter colonies that will hopefully be strong colonies in 2014. He literally has to rebuild his honeybee population from scratch.

Phil has his Masters in Philosophy. Peter and I were fortunate to be invited to his Masters defence – his thesis was titled "Honeybees and Consciousness." Phil is gentle and generous with his time and sharing his knowledge of beekeeping. His guidance has been part of why I have a successful career. Phil, the scientists, their ideas, their books, papers and their giving of time are definitely part of my history.

As is Gary Hooper, a high school English teacher and hobby beekeeper from St. Rose du Lac, Manitoba, who gave me the first lesson on creating text within the hive, thereby convincing me that I could sculpt collaboratively with the honeybees.

As are Henry and Rita Funk, the beekeepers with whom I worked and tested ideas related to honeybee construction abilities – for several autumn seasons. In their honey house I saw ... well, can you imagine using new pantyhose as a sieve to strain honey through? Brilliant idea and an image of a pair of pantyhose strained to the limit with wax bits, oozing honey was a sight to behold and never to forget. I do not know if the health inspector approved ... even though packages of unopened pantyhose were on a shelf in the honey house. Those type of sights and inventive ideas filter or de-filter an artist's mind. At least they did mine.

2. Dialogues

Haladyn—An interesting thing that has come up in our discussions is the history of interactions or collaborations you engage in through your practice. Do you see this as an important aspect of your art?

Dyck—Collaboration can be an important aspect in my work, especially when collaborating with an artist who works in a medium that differs from mine. When William Eakin, Richard Dyck and I collaborated on *The Wax Museum* we had great discussions, it was very exciting to work with each other, and each of us saw 'ideas, suggestions and materials' differently.

    Collaboration is important to my practice with the honeybees and it delves further into my thinking of the environment and the possible extinction of honeybees and the other living beings of the world. As humans, we might want to seriously consider collaborating with each other and with our environment, with the *small of the world*, if we wish the world to stay suitable and sustainable for all living beings. Other than the many human languages of the world, there are creatures around us who are surely trying to communicate with us, as they are communicating with each other. I am excited about the renewed interest in the language of plants – perhaps that is where to begin a conversation.

I have been greatly influenced by Mark L. Winston while in his bee lab. He was open to collaboration – in fact he encouraged the discussion of ideas with other disciplines and with other faculty members. Mark is an amazing, fun loving, passionate and generous human being. Mark's Honeycomb Project is an effort to inspire faculty members across Simon Fraser University to deliver interdisciplinary, community based and experiential learning. He says (I paraphrase, this is not a direct quote) "that the honeycomb is a place of great communication, idea transmission and collaboration between the different faculties and perspectives that each individual brings to the table."

Having shared the above, I also need quiet times, undisturbed times to research, think and experiment: to play with ideas and to focus.

Haladyn—You seem to enjoy engaging in dialogues with people in various fields, such as scientists and beekeepers, even the scholars you read and from which you get some of the images in your drawings. All these interactions form a type of network that informs your practice. In our discussion, for example, you consistently talk about the people who have supported you and who you interact with in order to create work. How do these connections inform your artistic practice?

Dyck—I can only imagine that it is the other people's way of thinking, their ideas, their sharing of knowledge and at times their use of materials and mediums,

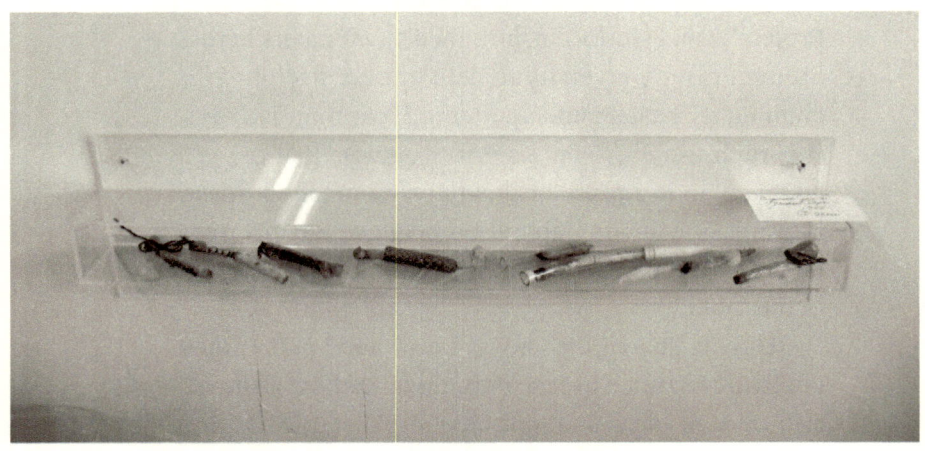

75. *Altered Cigarettes and Cigars*, 1988
view in Dyck's studio
photograph by Miriam Jordan-Haladyn

plus their very way of being that inform my artistic practice. My artwork happens due to my connection with any living being that allows me to enter their realm. I use their abilities to speak, use their products to construct and transform ideas. I hope that my artwork relates to interconnectedness, that it leads others to join in a dialogue.

I think working within several disciplines, working with individuals or groups who use various mediums and disciplines creates and expands dialogue. Especially if I ask for the public's participation. In simple terms, collaboration is an interconnection during which one cannot escape dialogue – whether verbal or visual.

I know that the work with cigarettes created dialogue as I was working on the project. Letters, photographs, questions from participants – mainly due to the fact that I had requested participation from individuals who wanted to quit the smoking habit. The participants sent me their last cigarette along with a letter – the letter could speak about anything at all, mainly they spoke regarding their reasons for wanting to quit the smoking habit. This project created dialogue between exhibitions dealing with the subject and during each exhibition.

At the time of this exhibition, *Hand Held: Between Index and Middle Finger*, the national press was constantly discussing cigarettes as well as how the tobacco companies were supporting art projects, movies, charitable organizations, etc. – one support that comes to mind was their support for musical festivals and events. The tobacco companies and the music industry were continuously supporting each other – sort of – until the public dialogue ended the relationship.

Haladyn—I am also thinking of your connections with history, including art history. You have mentioned your interest in the work of Joseph Beuys several times and I was hoping you could elaborate a bit. Can you describe your interest in his work? Are there specific artworks that you enjoy or have informed your practice?

Dyck—Joseph Beuys is a mystery to me – as it seems he is to many critics and art historians. During my three week residency in Banff, years ago, an art student who was tanning on the lawn of Banff's student's residency called as I walked by. She asked if I wanted her book on Beuys. It had rained and she had left the book outside and it was damp and the pages were stuck together. I did not know her, nor did we exchange names, she just gave me this big book, saying: "Please keep it." It was meant to be. I believe it is one of his 'catalogues' filled with black and white images of his felt works, his honey pump, his time living with a wolf – his time in America. I did take the book and dried it out page by page ... I was working with felt at the time and this book looked like a felted book, still does.

    Prior to taking part in Kunst and Complex studio in Rotterdam I had been drawing with ink the colour of amber, or the colour of propolis – the honeybee's glue that the bees use to fill cracks and openings in their hives to make it draft free. The drawings were very loose and flowing, not very interesting is what I thought and I did not keep them. I thought of them as an exercise.

    At that time I did not believe that I could draw and was embarrassed about my drawings, mostly

145

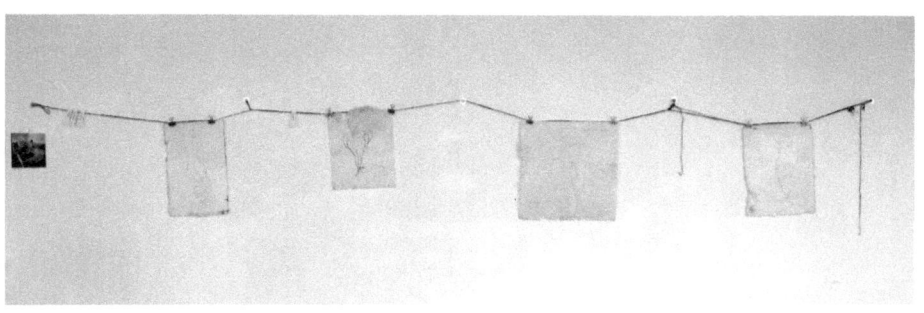

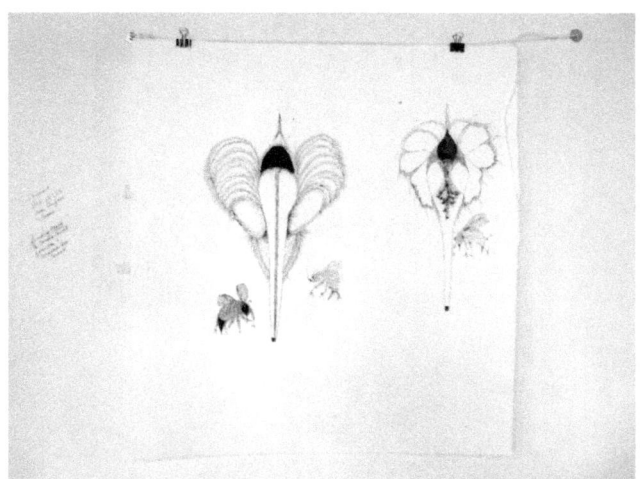

76-77. View of Dyck's drawings on the wall in her studio, 2010

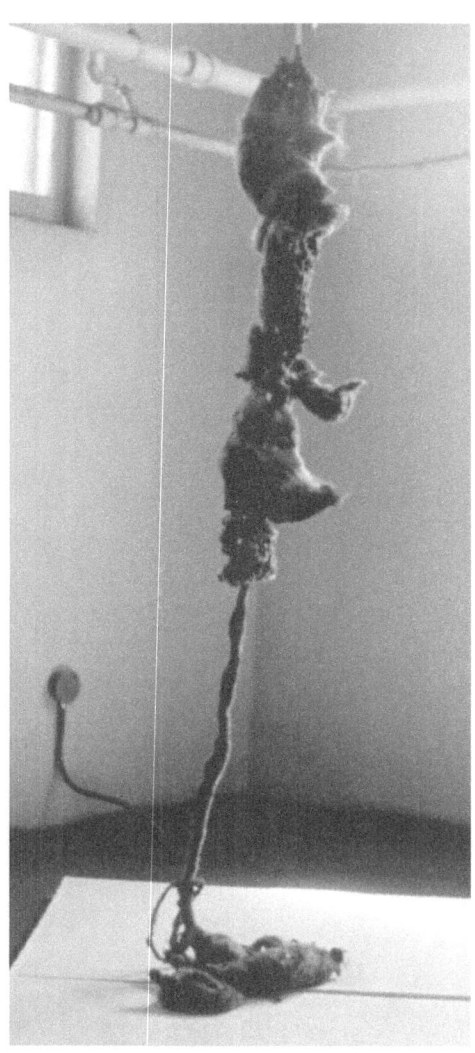

78. *Shrunken Sculpture*, 1976
photographs by Peter Dyck

hiding them from visitors – and destroying them as soon as possible.

During my travels to visit the Louvre and the Pompidou I purchased two books on Beuys. Alain Borer and Lothar Schirmer's *Joseph Beuys: Eine Werkubersicht* and the other *Thinking is Form: The Drawings of Joseph Beuys* by Ann Temkin and Bernice Rose. I was so surprised to see he used stain, fat and oil for many of his drawings, such as the *Life of the Bees* (1954 and 1956) and *Bienenkoenigen* (1952) – the latter is a drawing that was very close to how I drew honeybees using amber coloured inks. His work was exciting to me, it allowed me to become a bit freer in the studio.

From 1976 to 1981, when I was felting discarded woolen clothing by the hundreds, my mentor George Glenn, an art professor at Prince Albert's Community College, told me about Beuys. George talked to me about felt and especially about Beuys and his felt suit. I saw Beuys' felt wall sculptures in 1997 while in residency in Britain.

I have been influenced by Georgia O'Keefe and her paintings of flowers, especially during one trip to New York when I saw a 'real' painting by her, quite startling to say the least. I could see deep into her flowers and was hooked, never to see a flower the same way again.

Haladyn—Can you expand a bit on your interest in Georgia O'Keefe's work?

Dyck—Georgia O'Keefe was one of my role models in the mid 1970s when my career was just beginning. I was inspired by her determination and her tenacity – by her way of creating art 'her way' and not following practices of conventional art making.

I always thought of art as a visual language and when I read that O'Keefe thought of art as a language, I felt validated. Her paintings of skeletons reminded me of her flowers, and her flowers appeared to morph into skeletons, even though the skeletons were mostly rendered in white or grey and the flower paintings were mostly painted using vivid colours. O'Keefe is one of my heroes of the art world.

Haladyn— Marcel Duchamp's name has also come up in relation to your work a few times – Juan Antonio Ramirez wrote an essay directly comparing your "Bride" to Duchamp's. Do you see a connection between his work and yours?

Dyck—In the 1970s I was introduced to Duchamp's work during an art class, as well as by George Glenn. When I first used found objects in my work, George pointed me to Duchamp. Duchamp gave artists, me included, permission to use found objects and materials not usually associated with art making. I find Duchamp's work mysterious and humorous at the same time.

Haladyn—Is there a particular aspect of his practice that interests you?

Dyck—I particularly like Duchamp's *Fountain*. I find this readymade a most humorous and smart idea, work. *The Bride Stripped Bare by Her Bachelors* is a work I need to read up on. I found this work very dark, very full of angst and that probably has nothing to do with Duchamp's intent.

Haladyn—What do you think of Duchamp's "The Creative Act"?

Dyck: When I first read "The Creative Act" I thought "Of course!" ... without qualifying ... Of course bad art is still art ... Of course the spectator has something to say whether an artist is successful or becomes famous or if an artist's work stands the test of time. The public and commercial art world is involved in bringing an artist to the forefront or ignoring the artist's work so that it disappears from considerations.

You ask what I think of Duchamp's lecture, exactly that. I think about it, but also mentally stumble when trying to understand it. I know that I do not know enough to comment further in any intellectual level.

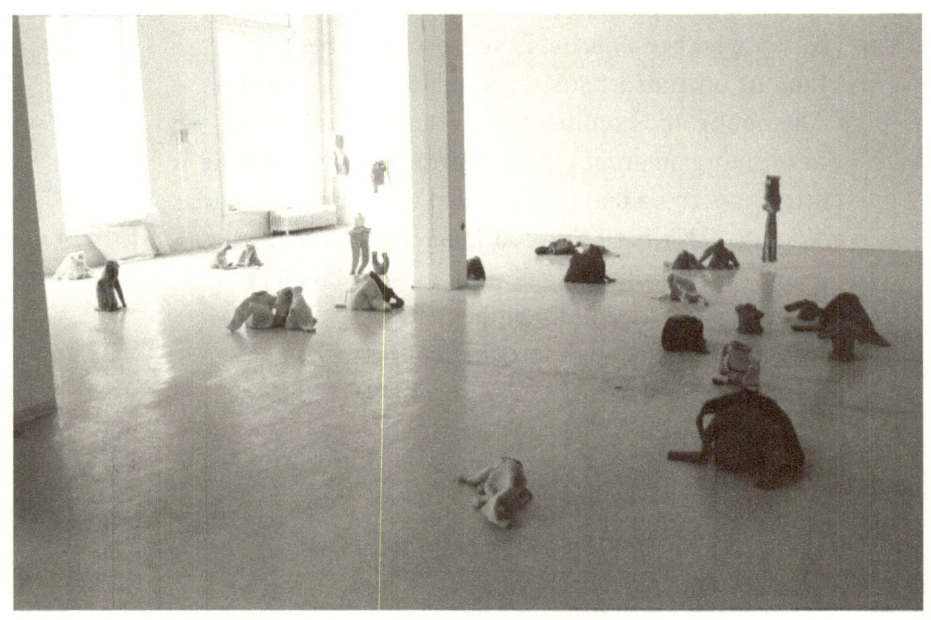

79. *Sizes 8 – 46*, 1978
    installation view in Arthur Street Gallery (now Plug In Gallery of Contemporary Art)

3. Small and Large

Haladyn—How would you characterize your overall interest in small things?

Dyck—My first mentor suggested that I might consider working large as well as working small, since both can be powerful. This while I was shrinking clothing, creating a series titled *Sizes 8 – 46*. I thought that was what I was doing: taking large garments and shrinking them until they would not shrink anymore. The shrunken clothing turned into a large installation.

Haladyn—There is a fantastic phrase you have repeatedly used to describe your interest in working with the bees: 'the power of the small'. Do you believe that your idea of 'the power of the small' can be applied to your work before the bees?

Dyck—I had never thought of 'power of the small' as being part of my work prior to the honeybees. Julian, you are making me think again!
    Including the over 600 articles of shrunken garments – it was both large and small. The installation was actually huge, even though the objects of shrunken clothing were small. I am thinking

especially of the shrunken toques in *Hockey Night in Canada* ... cup size toques that once covered quite large heads. This body of work from 1976-81 still holds interest and is still being exhibited and collected, albeit in 'small groups' of clothing.

Haladyn—Just like you I also thought about the shrunken hats and sweaters – one of my favourite series of your works – but also the buttons and cigarettes. And yes, many of your installations are big ... with lots of canned buttons or displays of altered cigarettes. But this bigness is based on an accumulation or collection of small things that add up, or are contained – I am also thinking about the suitcases. What is it about these small objects that attracts you?

Dyck—I am not so certain that small objects have attracted me prior to the precious, smallness and importance of the honeybees. Much of the small in my work, prior to the honeybees 'kind of presented itself' ...

By my renting a studio filled with buttons, waist high, from a manufacturer of buttons, zippers and thread. In the late 1970's I was part of a shared studio on the 4th floor of 376 Donald Street. I wanted to move out because I required more space, but my budget did not allow for extra studio rent. One day, a well dressed business man was coming down the studio building stairs as I was walking up the stairs; he stopped me and asked if I was an artist and if I required studio space and could he show me the 5th floor that he wanted to sublet. I followed him up to the 5th floor to see the space filled with his stash of millions of buttons. I was instantly interested in the space and in the buttons. He said he was moving out and did not want the buttons either. I could hardly breath, I was so overwhelmed at this opportunity. He rented me the space on the spot and also sold me all the buttons.

However, I did not have the $500 he wanted for the buttons. Without hesitating I went to the bank just down the street where Peter was a customer. I asked to see the bank's loans manager. The loans officer's secretary asked if I had an appointment – I did not. For some reason the manager noticed that his secretary was obviously trying to make an appointment and I think the he wondered who I was, perhaps my 'artist garb' made him curious. He opened his door and said something to his secretary, all the while looking at me. He beckoned me to come in, to sit down, to have a coffee and then asked what I needed. I told him my story and he listened with great interest that I needed $500 to purchase the buttons. He asked if I had collateral – yes, half ownership in a home. Did I have a car? I told him that Peter and I had a car. He asked for my husband's phone number and called Peter at work, asking if Peter would co-sign a loan for me. Peter informed him that he saw no reason why he needed to co-sign my loan. The manager smiled and nodded. I signed for the loan and the next day the button manufacturer was paid in full. The best part of this story is that I sold a work for $600 the next week and paid off my loan.

The studio was 3600 sq. ft. and, to help with the rent and utilities, I required a co-renter. A few evenings later our friends, who are involved in Mennonite Theatre productions, came for dinner; they said the theatre company had been given notice to move out of the theatre's studio space. To make a long story short, the theatre company rented half the 5th floor at 376 Donald Street. Because the theatre group only worked evenings, I had the space to myself during the day (*perfect!*).

I did purchase the stash of buttons, not knowing what to do with this merchandise. I began trading buttons for art supplies and even for home baking when I required baking for special events, baking for the family. The idea of millions of buttons attracted visitors to my studio – artists and curators and friends of friends. These visits allowed for dialogue and ideas of what to do with them to be suggested freely, everything from: 'glue them all over your clothing' to 'glue them all over your walls' – mostly ideas on how to *glue* the buttons to something. When my friend Winona Senner from Prince Albert Saskatchewan came to visit she suggested I bake a button pie. I did that and nearly burned our house down; fortunately our son grabbed the fire extinguisher and put out the oven fire. Sometimes I just do not stop to think ...

This led to experimenting with ideas of food preparation for the home. I began to think of the pioneers who settled in this country and how they laboured growing food, and how they preserved food for the winter months. How did they manage to survive all the harshness of this land?

In fall, a few years after owning the buttons, I thought of preserving food for the winter. My mother was canning amazing preserves, her basement looked fantastic with all the basement shelving filled with colours: tomatoes, pickles, mustard relishes, vegetables, fruit, jams and jellies. Cupboard after cupboard filled with glistening jars of preserves, just like at my grandparent's house. Influence up close and

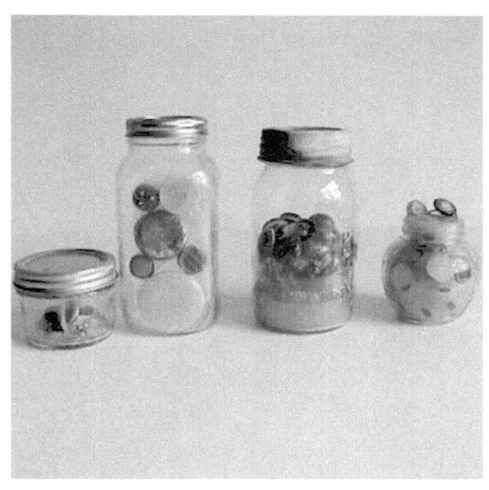

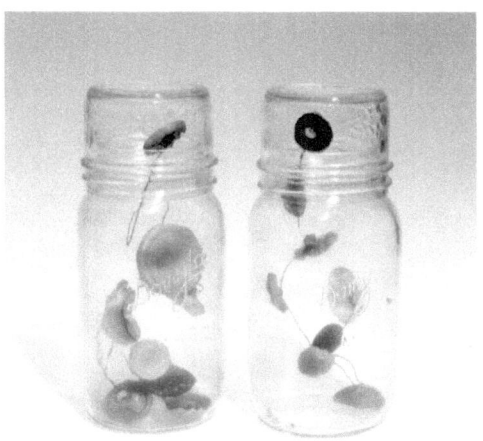

80-81. *Canned Buttons*, 1984
photograph by Sheila Spence

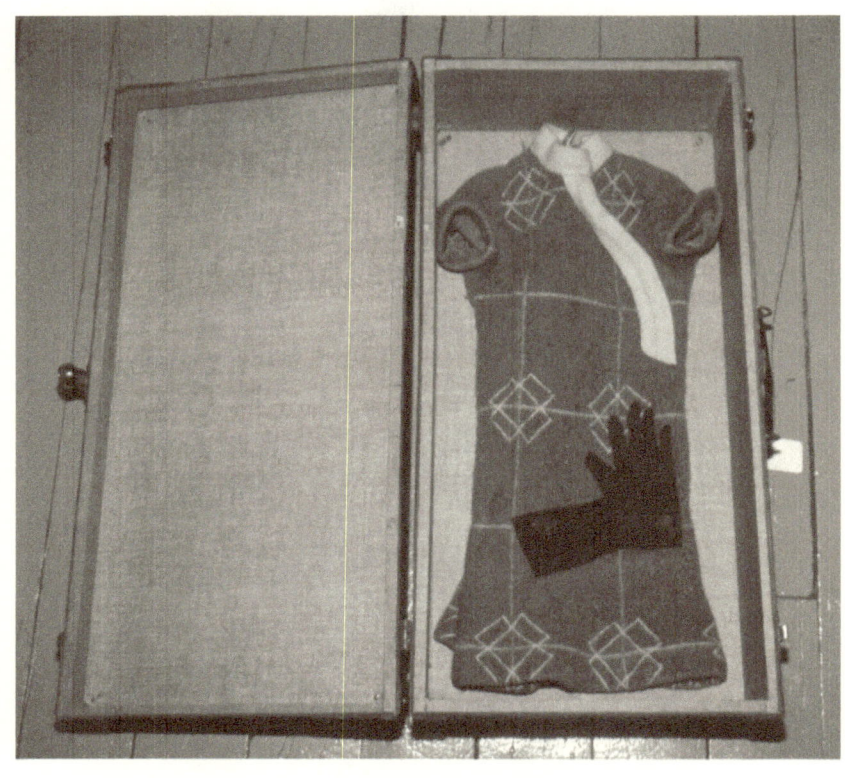

82. *Shrunken Dress in Suitcase*, 1978-81
 photograph by William Eakin

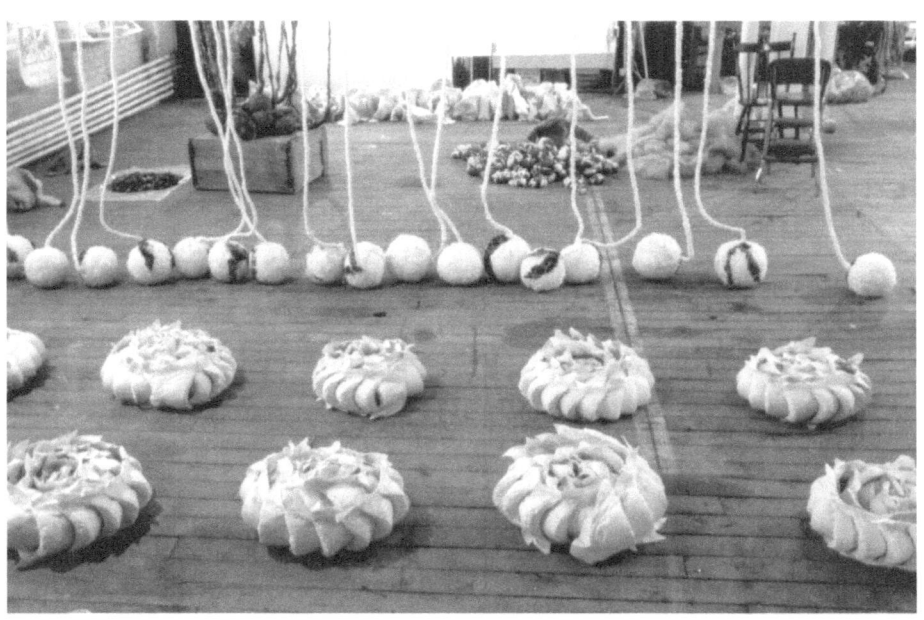

83. *Cabbages*, 1978 [in foreground]
view of Dyck's 376 Donald studio
photograph by William Eakin

personal, you might say. Plus the boxes of buttons were getting weak from age and were breaking, flooding small areas of my studio. I gathered them with a broom and a small plastic shovel and stored them in jars – large jars that a restaurant was giving away.

The cigarettes became an 'attraction' or a 'material' requiring a medium to alter the cigarette's suggested use. It began with a conversation I had with two young artists sitting on the outer steps of a Winnipeg building, they told me how difficult it was to stop their smoking habits. They had tried acupuncture, hypnosis, medications, all to no avail. I asked them for their cigarettes, offering to alter the cigarettes for them so that they could not smoke them anymore. I returned the altered cigarettes to them soon after altering them in my studio. That started a small landslide of requests from people wishing to stop their smoking habits and this in turn became a project.

The suitcases were actually an idea for the studio's storage of materials. The shrunken clothing required storage – one thing led to another. The suitcases, except for one, were ruined in our home basement storage area due to the city's sewer system backing up ... this occurrence actually ruined *cabbages* as well. It ruined much of my early archives.

Haladyn—Do you enjoy the chance encounters?

Dyck—I enjoy chance encounters that lead me to create a project. Chance encounters are always a welcome surprise, even though they can interrupt a project in progress. For example, I am nearing the end of a project when another 'chance encounter' arrives that is exciting and alters the project in a big way. This means further research, decision-making and at times a total redesign of an idea.

During the canning of the buttons, in the 1980s, I required wax for sealing the canned button jars. I was purchasing beeswax from Bee Maid honey, a beekeeper's supply house, when I looked up and saw an interesting sign with text that read 'BEE MAID'. I enquired regarding the text and was informed it was created by honeybees: it was text with honeycomb, approximately 6 inches deep and 20 inches long. It was 'chance at first sight'. I discovered that Gary Hooper of St. Rose du Lac, Manitoba – who was a high school English teacher and was a hobby beekeeper – that he and his honeybees had created the sign. He and his honeybees produced honey and wax plus they created text within his hives for the joy of it, I think.

I was given Gary's phone number and called him the next day, asking if he would teach me what he knew about honeybees and especially how he had his bees create the 'BEE MAID' honey sign. He invited Peter and I to visit. We spent a day sitting at his kitchen table discussing honeybees and their construction abilities. Gary was most generous with his time and knowledge, I would not have thought it possible to create with honeybees had Gary not shared his amazing talent ... and had he not given the Bee Maid manager the honeycombed sign.

Discovering that the honeybees were sculptors ended the canning of buttons. I cleaned up my studio, stored former art works and began researching honeybees. Knowing that the honeybees were sculptors and since I was a sculptor, it made sense we could collaborate. Not ever having been around

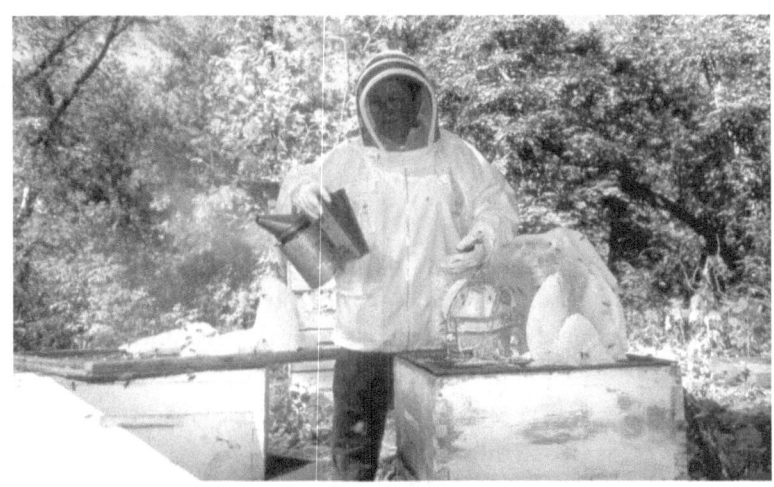

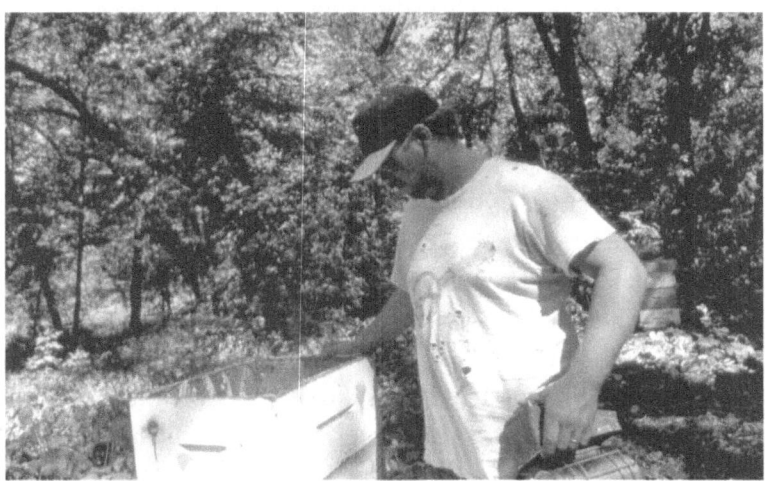

84. Dyck and bees with *Sports Night in Canada* [football helmet], 1995

85. Phil Veldhuis inspecting beehive, 1995
    St. Norbert Arts and Cultural Centre Apiary
    images courtesy of Aganetha Dyck

honeybees, not knowing a beekeeper was the only stumbling block. I would begin beekeeping research at Winnipeg's main library in the morning.

The first day of research at Winnipeg's main library, I met Louise May and a friend who were part of the organization of St. Norbert Arts and Cultural Centre, in St. Norbert, a suburb of Winnipeg. They asked why I was borrowing books on honeybees; I told them the story about Gary Hooper and that I wanted to find a beekeeper near Winnipeg to see if he or she would work with me. Louise informed me that a young beekeeper had just placed his hives on St. Norbert Arts and Cultural Centre's yard and did I want to meet him? I visited the apiary and met Phil Veldhuis. We talked and he said he would like to try what I was proposing. Phil gave me a few lessons on 'how to behave around honeybees' and told me that next time we went in the apiary I could bring something for the bees to experiment with. I purchased a bee suit, a bee smoker and a hive tool and met Phil a few days later. Phil shared information about beekeeping and bee behaviour. We began an amazing work relationship that spanned 20 years.

Phil has his Masters of Philosophy degree. He invited Peter and I to attend his Masters defence, which we did. Phil took a chance on me and because of his amazing gift of teaching I became a collaborator with honeybees. Every spring Phil created a new apiary studio for me to create art with the honeybees. Peter constructed special hives for each project.

Haladyn—That is amazing. These chance events have obviously played a key role in role in your practice, especially in terms of discovering the bees ... 'chance at first sight' as you said. Do you see chance playing a specific role in your approach to art making?

Dyck—I use chance in my creation of projects by trial and error with material use, with ways of working.

A few years ago I forgot to remove my still warm iron from a sheet of comics that had been wrapped around a big block of wax. A beekeeper had wrapped his wax block in comics for shipment. I noticed wax melting through the comics and removed the iron. At this moment I received a phone call and left to answer. After the phone call, I noticed that the comic's wax surface had hardened and I had to peel the comics off the block of wax. A print of the comics remained on the wax block. I did many experiments with my iron and imprinting onto beeswax after that and created a series of wax tiles using this technique.

I actually think most artists work with chance or because of chance. We discover new ways of working, we develop new material use, we invent techniques, we develop tools for specific projects. We observe and often see solutions 'by chance' and we use chance for what suits our needs and purposes. I am thinking of photography; all the inventions that have happened because of an idea, a need, a chance discussion with a friend or stranger. And a painter surely 'happens' on a new method of working ... surely one paint falls into another and colours mix or textures form. Chance happenings are a regular occurrence in life, don't you think? If we only take the time or have the luxury to take the time, we can often benefit from chance encounters of the most unlikely and unexpected type and kind. I think of inventors and scientists who come upon an idea 'out of the blue', so to speak, and discover amazing ways of working and invention.

Haladyn—I am struck by your description of chance as functioning, in a sense, as an important basis for cultural creation, which you suggest is not limited to the artistic. While I might be going a bit too far with this question, I would really love to hear what you understand 'art' to be, both personally and culturally?

Dyck—Your question is a great one and yes, a big one! I could not answer that in 'one gulp' so to speak.

I feel that I understand art on a personal level working with honeybees ... and have understood art on a personal level with all my projects. I see art as a language, as a thought process or as a medium for investigations that feed my curiosity, a way of asking questions of others wherever and whenever there is a possibility to dialogue.

I want to share with you my response to questions Dr. Mark L. Winston asked of me last week. Mark is writing a new book on 'lessons learned from the bees'. He is so pleased to be working with his ideas of his beloved bees! Understandable. These answers relate to the section of his new book on the 'art and spirituality':

1) Honeybees inspire me to work with them because they feed my curiosity. They allow me to experiment, they lead me into new and fruitful directions. Honeybees teach me to think into their box and out of my box. Honeybees have and continue to inspire designers, architects and artists throughout the world. Honeybees have

definitely enlarged my imagination by sharing possibilities and by observing their methods of hive construction in trees, in boxes, suspending their swarms on a tree branch, by cuddling the Queen, by balling the Queen, by being 'in the dark' and by their mysterious languages.

2) The honeybees are my muse because they allow me to contemplate, to wonder and reflect on who is this truly mysterious, magical, gift giving pollinator? A honeybee shares creativity and that is the best collaborative idea I received from observing the honeybees. All my work with the honeybees has been a 'give and take' of ideas.

3) Spirituality in my work? I can only say that I feel alive when entering the world of these ancient beings of wisdom. Spending time in the honeybees' world opens a new world of wonder for me. Being with the honeybees makes my ordinary life stand still and makes time disappear. When working with the honeybees, their warmth surrounds me, I feel like I am in a bubble of caring. I feel connected to the ancients, to wisdom and to collaboration. The honeybees taught me to understand that I was part of the global environment. I have meditated while in the apiary on many occasions and felt that my meditation was being shared.

4) Honeybees are responsible for my increased imagination as an artist by sharing their imagination when I put an object into their hives. The honeybees followed the object's contours,

closed openings, opened closures on thin, solid surfaces such as on paper and on wax tablets. They created straight lines of comb where I would never have thought it possible or necessary. Since working with honeybees I am open to being influenced by many more avenues that circumvent the world I live in. Opening a hive for the first time is similar to traveling to a strange, new country. The sights and scents, the sounds and warmth, the movement – these are rare discoveries of any new space, including the space in which honeybees choose to make their home.

5) Honeybees helped me become more responsible for the world I live in. Honeybees are responsible for exciting dialogue and new collaborative possibilities with others. Every exhibition that deals with honeybees brings new and positive connections for which I am very thankful.

And I did tell Mark that my imagination went wild when he gave me the gift of spending time in his Simon Fraser University lab. I told him that the time spent in his lab made me dizzy and that what I learned still makes me dizzy at times, when remembering the ideas he shared. I have used his ideas in my work as well as the ideas brought forth from his assistant, Heather Higo and students. It felt awesome being so close to all the knowledge and creativity in the lab that these ideas have stayed with me to this day. Mark is one of the most generous people I know. He has a great sense of humour and a calmness about him that defies definition. Perhaps his calmness comes from his life's work with honeybees.

Haladyn—The issue of spirituality is a difficult one. And your answer seems to reflect this, especially in terms of relating the spiritual to the "ancient beings" that are the bees.

Dyck—The issue of spirituality is unbelievably difficult for me. After Mark wrote for my exhibition *Nature as Language* at University of Manitoba, I began searching for the meaning of spirituality in art ... not even close to being able to discuss this in depth.

Haladyn—In a sense, I am returning to your description of art as a language. I also really appreciated the way you talk about art as asking questions and as 'a possibility of dialogue'. How do you see your work functioning as a language or dialogue?

Dyck—My artwork functions as a visual language because it asks questions and creates dialogue without the use of text and without the sound of a spoken word. I think of all art as a language, a language of ideas and questions. Or are questions actually ideas? Recently, during a visit to the Inuit Art Vault at the WAG, a group of local artists saw the early and more recent art of the Inuit, art with amazing depth ... shape, colour, texture, juxtapositions. We had a positive experience imagining the stories, myths and the ideas that the Inuit were sharing via their art making, via their very way of being.

    I do not know how else to talk about the visual language ... working in the studio is the only way I know how to speak with a full voice.

Haladyn—I am curious what you personally find most fulfilling about the environment of the studio?

Dyck—Working in my studio means freedom to explore new ideas, it fulfills dreams and challenges ideas of what could be. It allows for experimentation and accidental happenings, it allows for quiet reading, researching and contemplation. My studio feels like a place of celebration of 'what if' and excitement is never far distant. I am most fortunate to have the separate space to work in, using any materials, trying any medium, without other daily interference. My studio mates, Di Thorneycroft and Reva Stone and I have been sharing the 4th floor for 22 years without getting in each other's way of being. It is amazing to enter my studio space and know that the 'mess' or organization is mine and mine alone, and no one cares or comments if things are dripping honey or wax is covering half the heavily papered floor. My studio is freedom, a place to play and ponder.

Earlier in my career I grew as an artist by working in a series of studios. I worked for 3 weeks in the fibre studio in Banff, 2 month at the studio at Kunst and Complex in Rotterdam, 2 months in the Yorkshire Sculpture Park in Britain and a 3 month residency in Troyes, France. Plus, of course, a week long stay in Dr. Mark L. Winston's bee lab. Each studio offered learning, new cultural experiences, networking and collaboration. Artist residencies and travel have been important for my growth as an artist.

I find it interesting that we artists living in 'isolated' communities, complain about the isolation, yet call our private studio spaces a solace and a place where we can work 'alone'. *Hmmm.*

4. New Work

Haladyn — Given that your practice has become inextricably linked with the bees for over 20 years, not being able to work with them directly anymore must be exceedingly difficult for you. How have you been dealing with this challenge?

Dyck — The first idea was not to weep. I had to try to overcome my sadness at leaving the honeybees. Not being able to go to the hives by myself was devastating. I had thought about hiring an assistant to work according to my plans, to work alongside my husband Peter.

    Deep down inside my mind, however, I knew the time for change had come, that perhaps the bee work was more about creating beautiful art works; that working with the honeybees was too easy for me, that perhaps I was not challenging myself anymore. What were the honeybees telling me by causing their sting to become life threatening? Their stings had never caused me any problems before, except for a bit of pain.

    I was sad that I would not be able to touch the honeybees with my bare hands. I would not be able to crouch down to observe the guard bees. You never know if a bee has landed on your bee suit ... and being stung behind your knees while crouching is not to be recommended! I would not be able to sit in the grass near the hive to see what the honeybees were discarding or to observe them taking flight, or observe guard bees defending their colony when a grasshopper or another invader was wanting to enter the hive. Was the invader in the guard's sight line? Was the guard agitated – telling sister guards to assist? Or did the guard whiff the scent of a possible intruder and send the scent into the hive – calling for assistance.

I would miss taking my hive tool to pry open the hive lid, listening for the sound of breaking the propolis barrier. Propolis is the honeybee's glue. The honeybees re-glue their hive boxes and hive lids after someone has opened the hive and after the lid is put back into place.

Lifting the hive lid is like entering another world, a foreign scent and sound surrounds you. The sounds and scents of a hive change depending on what is going on within the hive. A new Queen is piping? The honeybees are fanning the heat out of the hive or they are warming the hive with their bodies and with the beating of their wings? Are the honeybees contented or agitated?

Upon opening a hive near Vancouver, a beekeeper remarked: "Can you smell the wild flower honey?" I could not differentiate the scent one from the other that day. Beekeepers rely on the sound and scent of a hive for information on the health of the colony, on what the colony is about to do – as in the sound of a hive suggesting to swarm due to overcrowding or some other unhappiness.

Haladyn—When we first met in Winnipeg in 2010 your passion for the bees really struck me. While I have studied your work for some time, it was something quite different to understand how passionate of an artist you truly are. And you talked about the sadness you felt about the idea of no longer being able to experience the honeybees.

Dyck—To alleviate my sadness I thought of the meditative times I enjoyed during the shrinking of the woollen clothing in *Sizes 8 – 46*, which I did from 1976 to 1981. How I had searched thrift stores to select woollen clothing, while considering the shape certain articles of clothing would result in. I considered the construction of a garment ... how would it shrink? And the types of yarn used in the manufacture of a garment, as in wool and rabbit fur or wool and silk or alpaca and wool. What would happen in the wash? And how an old-fashioned wringer washer would alter the clothing in a day or in a week of washing the same garments? When would a garment not shrink anymore?

    At the end of every studio washday the clothing was left to drip dry. The next morning the clothing was inspected and either accepted as shrunken or tossed back into the washer. Or perhaps it would disintegrate due to an infestation of wool moths that I had not noticed?

    And I thought of all the meditating, reading and researching that I did while the washer chug-chugged the garments into art ... the washer's sound and scent of Ivory laundry detergent became my mantra of sorts. My studio was a haven, visitors could relax and enjoy the atmosphere, the environment.

    After this 'remembering' of my very first body of work, I decided to revisit the clothing idea, to

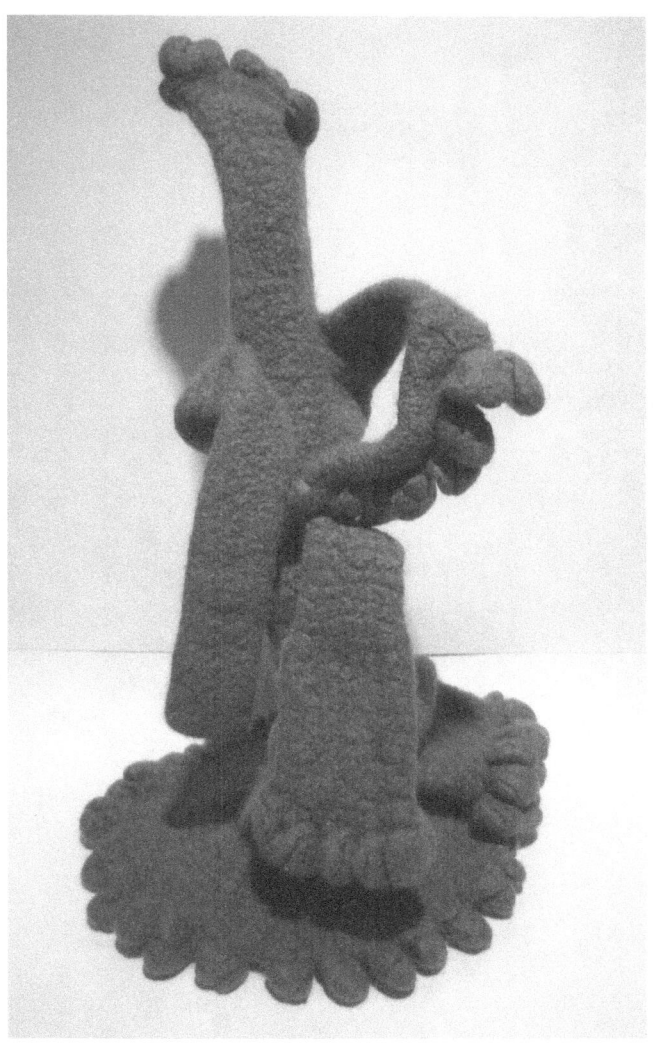

86. *Shrinks* (*Brown*), 2012
    image courtesy Michael Gibson Gallery

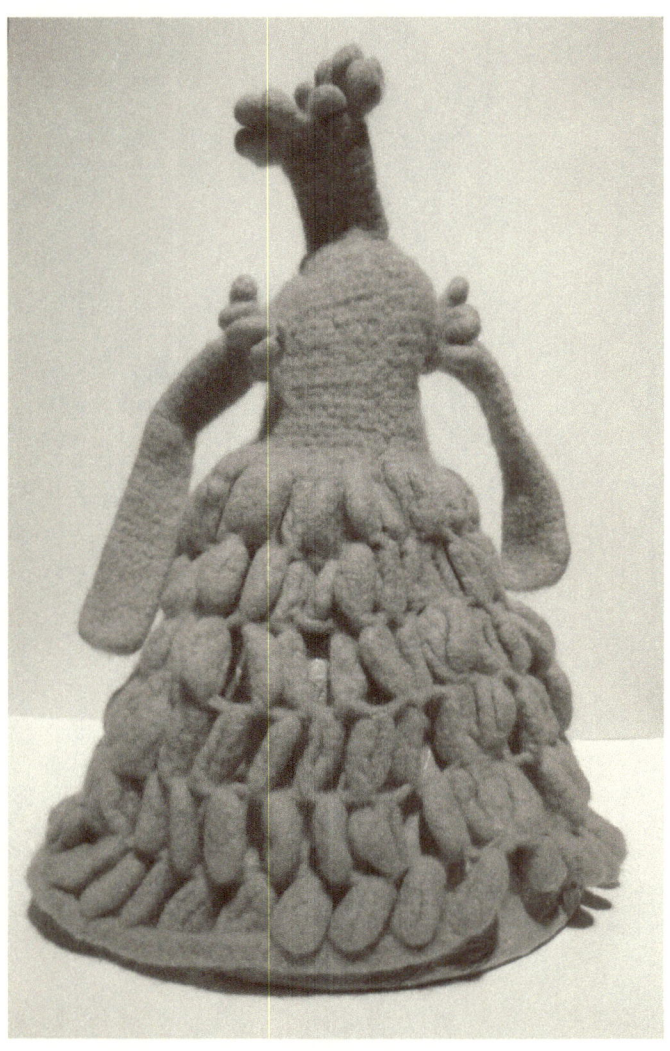

87. *Shrinks* (*Gold*), 2012
image courtesy Michael Gibson Gallery

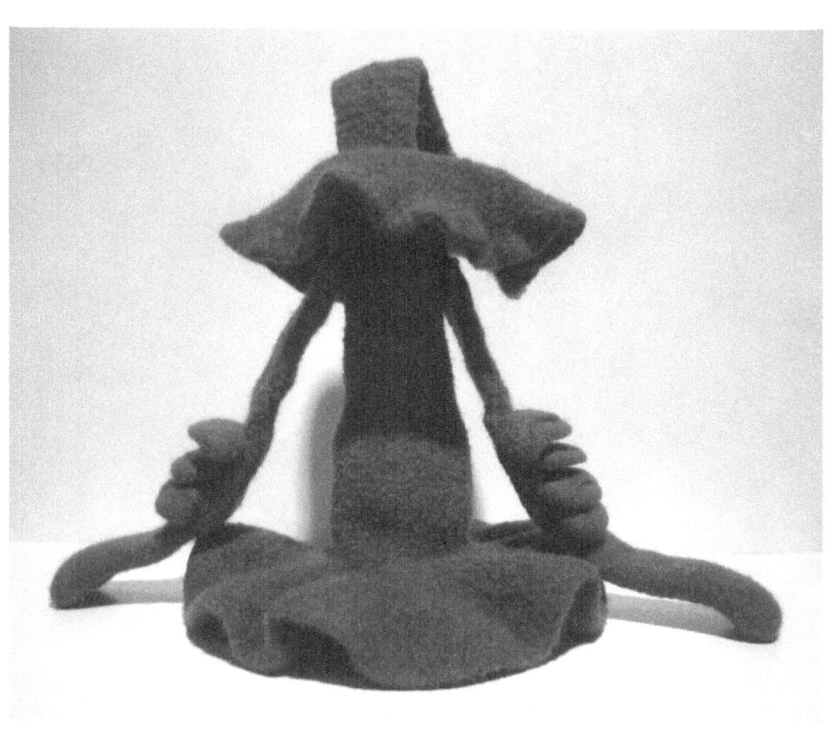

88. *Shrinks (Purple)*, 2012
image courtesy Michael Gibson Gallery

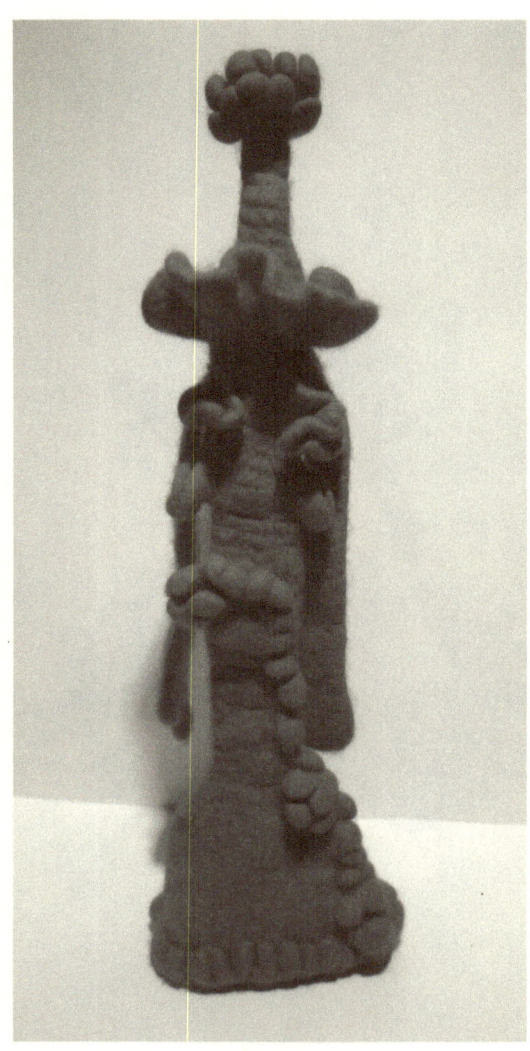

89. *Shrinks* (*Red*), 2012
    image courtesy Michael Gibson Gallery

design and crochet a series of 9 articles of clothing. I would crochet from my design concept and shrink the result. I researched designer clothing on and off the internet ... thought about it, purchased yarns and began crocheting. At times I drew my design idea on paper prior to crocheting, only to discover that is not how I work. Once freedom with the hook occurred, I simply crocheted and the clothing idea turned into 9 sculptures that I am told do not resemble clothing – at least not most of the time or for most viewers.

During the almost two years of crocheting, I decided not to leave the honeybees per se. Visiting and at times re-visiting beekeeper's honey houses and apiary workshops I began collecting old apiary materials and equipment. To date I have 180 very old hive blankets plus 117 equally old, well used feeder boards that contain waxed marks by the honeybees. A few have complete honeybee cells on them, others are only touched by the honeybees; yet others resemble hieroglyphics, codes left by the honeybees.

A curator recently viewed these finds and asked how I would use them, my reply was that I do not know. I am cleaning them by brushing and washing them, next I will fumigate them. It is a very exciting time as research on possibilities begins. And I do not have to 'leave the honeybees'. I can continue to work with them from afar, care about them and dream with wonder about these amazing pollinators.

Haladyn—What direction do you see your work taking in the next few years?

Dyck—This is definitely a new direction for me, *sans* direct contact with the honeybees. The apiary's by-products and beekeeper's workshop supplies are slowly filling my studio.

I recently met with beekeeper Art Veldhuis, Phil Veldhuis's father, who reconstructs damaged hives and hive parts in Phil's apiary workshop. Art showed me sections of hive frames that he has to replace; these slender parts have bee marks on them, they are hive frame 'sides'. Art is now saving me all sorts of hive parts that he has to replace ... I am so excited about this find!

At the moment I am working towards an exhibition at the Tom Thomson Gallery in Owen Sound, which will take place around 2015 or 2016. For this exhibition I will be using the above finds and thinking of honeybee's CCD problems, scientists finds, success stories in saving bees, chemical companies that spray nicotinoids onto crops – these chemicals are being outlawed in some countries ... the internet is filled with dialogue about CCD and what to do to save the honeybees.

I am trying to keep informed on international beekeeping. I am re-researching ancient hives and becoming especially interested in the old idea of a leaf hive. Leaf hives were a failure as apiary equipment but lovely to look at. Beekeepers are always looking for hive improvements, the leaf hive was an idea developed many years ago. Beekeepers have thought (among other ideas) of giant hives, very large honeybee cells ... which would contain more honey? Circular hives, slender, long hives, cone shaped hives, cave and tree canopy beekeeping, wild bees, *et cetera et cetera*.

I think of glass hives, sound tracks, dark rooms, special lighting, a pull out information booth of feeder boards, ancient hive messages on hive blankets ... I

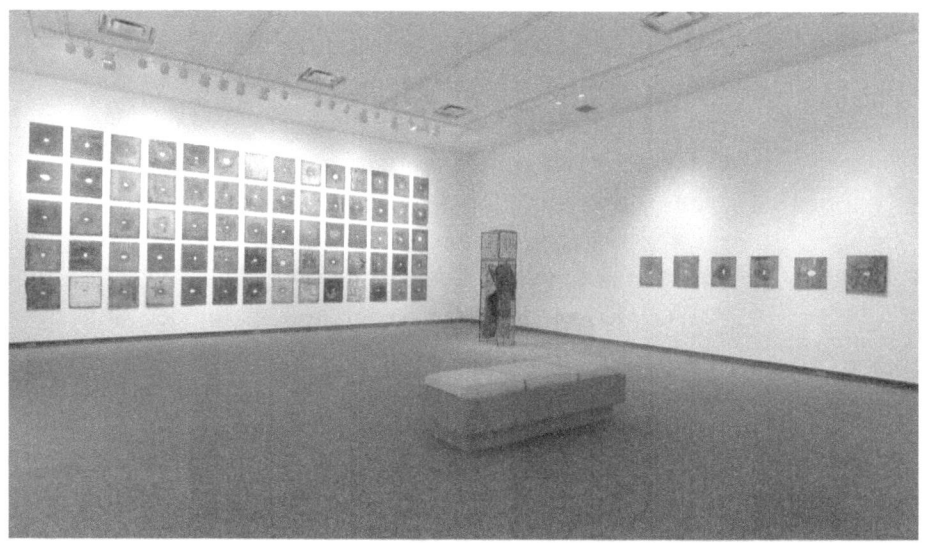

90. *Denouement: Memories of the Hive*, 2015
    installation view at Tom Thomson Art Gallery
    exhibition curated by Virginia Eichhorn
    photograph by Willy Waterton

see so many possibilities. Need to think clearly and edit down to one idea ...

Haladyn—The idea of working with old apiary materials sounds like the beginning of an amazing project.

Dyck—I will be cleaning 180 very old hive blankets and over 100 very old, wooden feeder boards that are waiting for me in our daughter's garage. Deb has offered space so I can work in the garage as well as outdoors in her yard. Living in an apartment is not a place for cleaning this material and my studio is also not conducive to handle so much crud! The cleaning is a dirty job, very time consuming. I think it will take me well over a month of scrubbing, making decisions of what to 'remove' as far as the honeybee's wax marks are concerned. After cleaning the work, it will be fumigated and brought up to my downtown studio for further decision-making.

    Cleaning very old and at times fragile apiary materials is something I need to do by myself. There are many decisions to be made and I do not want to lose the honeybee's codes of information during cleaning. I did hire our son to remove nails, screws and wooden framing from the feeder boards ... a mean job if ever there was one!

Haladyn—You sound quite excited about the task, which is wonderful. Do you have an idea of what you will do with this material once it is cleaned or will you come up with an idea while in the process of this work?

Dyck—Yes, I am excited about the supplies and discards from the apiaries! The resulting artwork is slated for

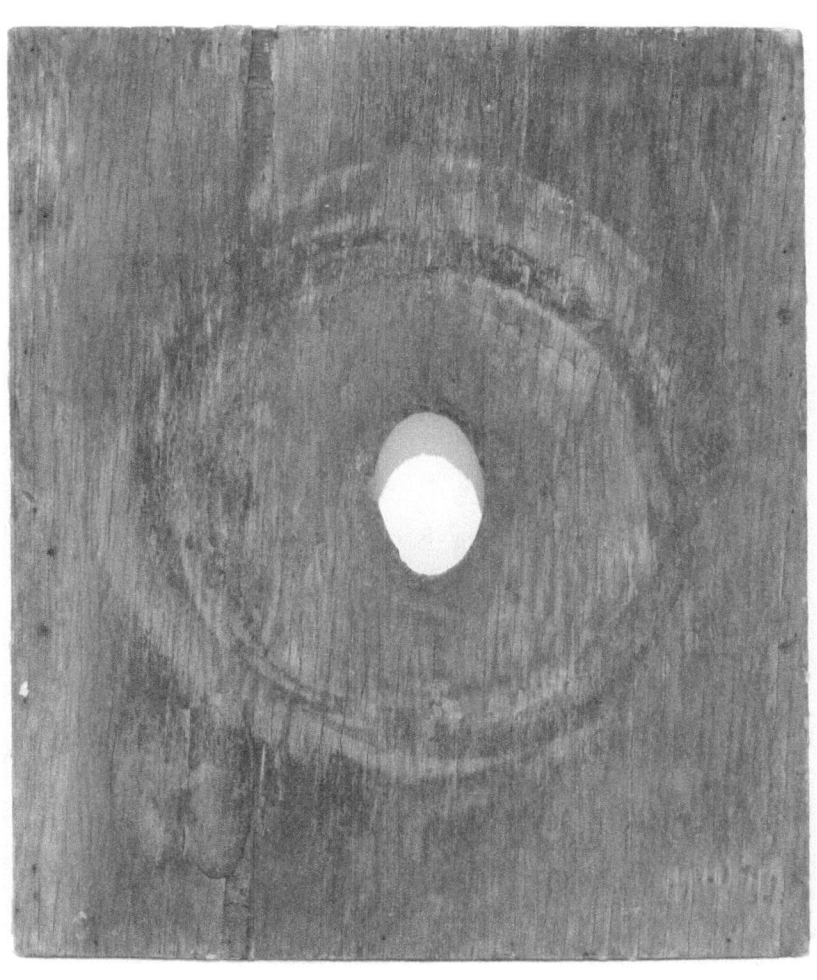

91. *Ancient Circle Print*, 2012-16
    image courtesy Michael Gibson Gallery

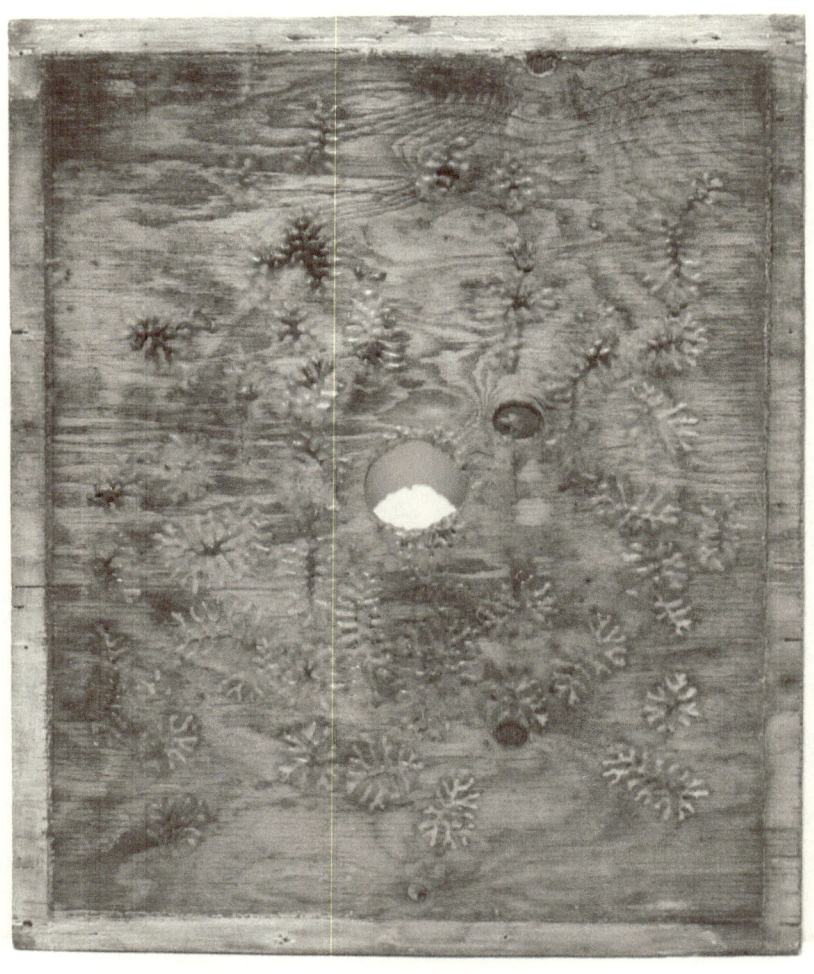

92. *The Apiary's Poem*, 2012-16
image courtesy Michael Gibson Gallery

the Tom Thomson Gallery. Curator Virginia Eichhorn and I are discussing possibilities. As you have probably noticed, the feeder boards on my website are beautiful as is: cleaned and fumigated. Now to do the same for my new stash.

I have collected the feeder boards and the hive blankets for 20 years. Having said that, the 180 blankets still to be cleaned were selected this summer. As intuition would have it, I called beekeepers Henry and Rita Funk's old honey house to see how they were doing. They were closing their beekeeping operation, had sold most of their beekeeping equipment. Our conversation led to an invitation for Peter and I to come see the Funks, talk a bit over lunch ... at Hadashville, Manitoba's Ukrainian restaurant that serves every type of perogy, sausage, and cabbage rolls imaginable.

We found the honey house quite bare except for pails of wild flower honey. Yes! We purchased honey: it is amazing. Depending on what type of wild flowers, the colours and tastes of their honey varies. It is rare to find so much organic wild flower honey.

In Funk's honey house, I noticed a pile of hive blankets on a shelf and was told they did not know what to do with them. I was ecstatic to say the least and offered to purchase them all. The Funks decided to keep 6 blankets as souvenirs of their beekeeping days. They asked what I wanted the blankets for and I had to say that I did not know. They remembered that in 1994 I had purchased a few dozen of their hive blankets and used them to sew the garments for *The Extended Wedding Party*.

This summer, Phil Veldhuis was altering his method of feeding his honeybees and was selling all his feeder boards ... there must be at least 1,000 boards in his storage shed. I took our daughter Deb with me to Starbuck, Manitoba and together we selected and purchased nearly 100 of these boards. Other than that, I have been selecting feeder boards for 20 years.

So here I am, thinking of what to do with these materials ... they are beautiful finds. A few of the feeder boards resemble hieroglyphics or codes yet to be cracked. Others leave marks, tracings or prints, of how honeybees create honeycomb. There is much to discover as I clean all these materials. As you suggest or ask: 'will you come up with an idea while in the process of this work?' That is definitely the plan. I am at the beginning of a new sculpture or installation project, many unknowns, much to ponder.

Haladyn—It is interesting to hear about a project you are just beginning. I am especially fascinated to hear about your working process, the sense of discovery and 'unknowns' you confront as you look at the things you have collected. Is this how you have worked when creating your previous projects?

Dyck—Yes, I always look at my collection of materials and begin investigating possibilities. An idea can change as time goes on. This way of working is difficult to explain. It is the only way I can work and is definitely part of my practice.

Haladyn— Given your concerns about not being able to work directly with the bees, it is wonderful to hear how pleased you are working in this manner. But cleaning of the apiary blankets and feeders must be really tough work.

Dyck—Yes, the cleaning is arduous. However, it is one great way of seeing the materials, noticing nuances and interesting bee marks that resemble codes or hieroglyphics. I will no doubt discover new areas of interest within the feeder boards as well.

A large wall of cleaned, slightly altered and fumigated feeder boards has been installed at Plug In Gallery for the (travelling) group exhibition *Toxicity*, co-curated by Melentie Pandilovski and Jennifer Willet – it opens this Friday, December 6th, 2013. I am totally pleased with this work, it is the best work by the honeybees ever and makes more sense to me than anything the bees and I have collaborated on in the past. Too early to speak about my thoughts at the moment, but I am very committed to proceed with other apiary finds.

Bill Eakin just documented the *Toxicity* exhibition and I am totally pleased with the installation. My work is receiving good responses.

Haladyn—Given your concerns about not being able to work directly with the bees, it is wonderful to hear how pleased you are working in this manner. What is it about these *apiary finds* (another great phrase!) that you find so rewarding?

Dyck—The latest apiary finds are strips of bee encrusted 'messages' that are part of hive frame sides. So far I have used these strips as 'signatures' for my new work. I used one strip to sign my latest embroidery, the one the beekeeper's son purchased ... he totally understood what the strip meant. We had a great conversation regarding Manitoba's huge bee losses in 2013. Scary, that.

Haladyn—You describe the strips of bee encrusted 'messages' as signatures. It is fascinating that a beekeeper's son could 'read' one of the strips. Again, we seem to be talking about these works in relation to the idea of language. In this case, working with these *apiary finds*, you seem to be investigating something that has already been 'written' and that you are in the process of uncovering.

Dyck—To answer your question, you will receive one of the honeybees' signatures to hang on your wall. The signatures are by and about honeybees, not so much about my work. These new works are truly only the *honeybee's work*. All I do is clean it and have it fumigated if necessary ... and put the work onto walls or as in the signature strips, they are placed next to one of my works ... perhaps it is a collaboration? I am just beginning this idea and cannot explain it at all. It feels right and keeps us, the bees and I, connected in my mind. If we were intelligent enough we possibly could read the marks made by the honeybees.

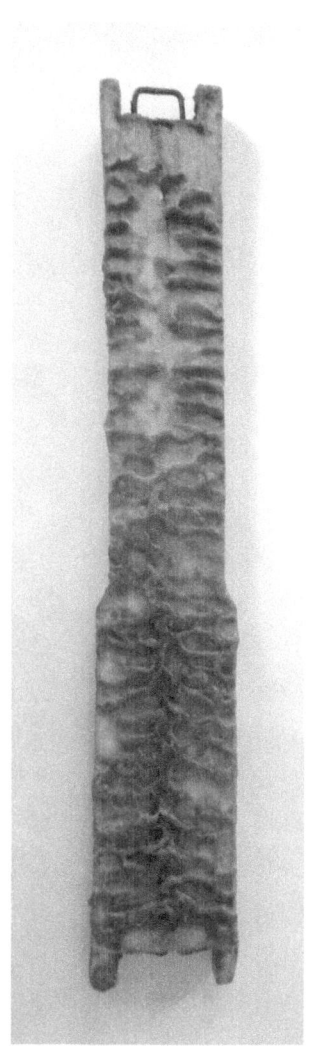

93. *Honeybees' Signature*, 2013

List of Figures

0. Honeybees working on *Sports Night in Canada* [baseball], 1995
    installation view at St. Norbert Arts and Cultural Centre Apiary
    live honeybees, sports equipment and beeswax on beehive boxes
    dimensions variable
    image courtesy of Aganetha Dyck
1. Aganetha and Peter Dyck's Garden at their house in Winnipeg, 2010
    photograph by Miriam Jordan-Haladyn
2. Aganetha and Jamelie Hassan in Dyck's studio, 2010
    photograph by Miriam Jordan-Haladyn
3. View of Dyck's studio, 2010
    photograph by Miriam Jordan-Haladyn
4. *Close Knit*, 1976-1981
    65 Shrunken Sweaters
    dimensions variable
    photograph by Peter Dyck
5. *Shrunken Clothing on a Road*, 1976-1981
    photograph by Peter Dyck
    dimensions variable
6. *Shrunken Clothing on a Road* (yellow sweater), 1976-1981
    photograph by Peter Dyck
    dimensions variable
7. *Shrunken Clothing on a Road*, 1976-1981
    photograph by Peter Dyck
    dimensions variable

8. *Merry Christmas Mr. Kooper*, 1981
     shrunken sweater and dominoes
     photograph by Elizabeth Legge
9. *Hockey Night in Canada*, 1981
     shrunken woolen toques
     dimensions variable
     photographs by Peter Dyck
10. *Hockey Night in Canada*, 1981
     shrunken woolen toques
     dimensions variable
     photographs by Peter Dyck
11. *Hockey Night in Canada*, 1981
     shrunken woolen toques
     dimensions variable
     photographs by Peter Dyck
12. *Large Cupboard* [detail of single unit], 1984
     installation view at Winnipeg Art Gallery
     glass jars, buttons and wax on wooden shelving units
     181 x 91 x 60 cm
     image courtesy Winnipeg Art Gallery
13. *Large Cupboard*, 1984
     installation view at Winnipeg Art Gallery
     glass jars, buttons and wax on wooden shelving units
     181 x 91 x 60 cm [each of the 10 shelving units]
     image courtesy Winnipeg Art Gallery
14. *Canning table*, 1984
     installation view at Winnipeg Art Gallery
     glass jars, buttons and wax on wooden table
     94.5 x 71 x 71 cm
     image courtesy Winnipeg Art Gallery
15. *Altered Cigarettes and Cigars* [details], 1988
     cigarettes and mixed media
     dimensions variable
     photographs by William Eakin

16. *Altered Cigarettes and Cigars* [details], 1988
    cigar and mixed media
    dimensions variable
    photographs by William Eakin
17. *Handheld: Between Index and Middle Finger*, 1988
    installation view
    cigarettes, cigars and mixed media in Plexiglas display case
    photograph by William Eakin
18. *Altered Cigarettes and Cigars*, 1988
    installation view in Dyck's studio
    cigar and mixed media in Plexiglas display case
    photograph by Miriam Jordan-Haladyn
19. *The Library: Inner / Outer*, 1991
    installation view at Southern Alberta Art Gallery
    mixed media, found objects and beeswax on wooden tables
    dimensions variable
    photograph by William Eakin
    collection of the Winnipeg Art Gallery
20. *Pages*, 1991
    installation view at Southern Alberta Art Gallery
    beeswax, found objects and record album on wooden shelves
    28 x 28 cm (each page), 15.1 x 290 x 35.3 cm (each shelf)
    photograph by William Eakin
    collection of the Winnipeg Art Gallery
21. *Pocket Book*, 1991
    evening bag, beeswax and found objects
    photograph by William Eakin
    collection of the Winnipeg Art Gallery
22. *Pocket Books for the Queen Bee*, 1991
    installation view at Southern Alberta Art Gallery
    evening bags, beeswax, found objects on two wooden tables
    dimensions variable
    photograph by William Eakin
    collection of the Winnipeg Art Gallery

23. *The Queen Bees's Telephone Directory*, 1991
    installation view at Southern Alberta Art Gallery
    beeswax, honey, yellow jackets and found objects on wooden table
    dimensions variable
    photograph by William Eakin
    collection of the Winnipeg Art Gallery
24. *Man's Shoes*, 1994
    shoes, pen and ink drawings, beeswax and honeycomb
    dimensions variable
    photograph by William Eakin
25. *Dance Shoes and Hive Blankets*, 1992
    installation view at Strike 3 Gallery
    shoes, drawings, beeswax and honeycomb on beehive boxes
    dimensions variable
    photograph by William Eakin
26. Honeybees working on *Lady in Waiting*, 1995
    installation view at Winnipeg Art Gallery
    live honeybees, beeswax and mixed media in Plexiglas container
    dimensions variable
    photograph by Sheila Spence
    image courtesy Winnipeg Art Gallery
27. *Extended Wedding Party*, 1995
    installation view at Winnipeg Art Gallery
    beeswax, glass, hive blankets, shoes and mixed media
    dimensions variable
    photograph by Sheila Spence
    image courtesy Winnipeg Art Gallery
28. *Extended Wedding Party* [detail of Bridesmaid's Dresses], 1995
    installation view at Winnipeg Art Gallery
    beeswax, hive blankets, shoes and mixed media
    dimensions variable
    photograph by Sheila Spence
    image courtesy Winnipeg Art Gallery
29. *Extended Wedding Party* [detail of *Groom*], 1995
    installation view at Winnipeg Art Gallery
    beeswax, hive blankets, shoes and mixed media

dimensions variable
photograph by Sheila Spence
image courtesy Winnipeg Art Gallery
30. *Extended Wedding Party* [detail of *Flower Girl* and *Bride*], 1995
installation view at Winnipeg Art Gallery
beeswax, glass, hive blankets, shoes and mixed media
dimensions variable
photograph by Sheila Spence
image courtesy Winnipeg Art Gallery
31. *Glass Dress: Lady in Waiting*, 1992-1998
installation view at the National Gallery of Canada
beeswax, glass and mixed media in Plexiglas container
dimensions variable
photograph by Peter Dyck
collection of the National Gallery of Canada
32. Dyck and Phil Veldhuis removing *Glass Dress* from beehive, 1995
installation view at St. Norbert Arts and Cultural Centre Apiary
image courtesy of Aganetha Dyck
33. Honeybees working on *Sports Night in Canada* [football helmet], 1995
installation view at St. Norbert Arts and Cultural Centre Apiary
live honeybees, sports equipment and beeswax on beehive boxes
dimensions variable
image courtesy of Aganetha Dyck
34. Honeybees working on *Sports Night in Canada* [fencing mask], 1995
installation view at St. Norbert Arts and Cultural Centre Apiary
live honeybees, sports equipment and beeswax on beehive boxes
dimensions variable
image courtesy of Aganetha Dyck
35. *Sports Night in Canada* [baseball hat and ball], 1995
sports equipment and beeswax on beehive boxes
dimensions variable
image courtesy of Aganetha Dyck
36. *Sports Night in Canada* [hockey stick and pucks], 1995
sports equipment and beeswax on beehive boxes
dimensions variable
image courtesy of Aganetha Dyck

37. *Sports Night in Canada* [football shoulder pads], 1995
    sports equipment and beeswax on wooden beehive boxes
    dimensions variable
    image courtesy of Aganetha Dyck
38. *Scientist*, 2007-2008
    view in Dyck's studio
    beeswax on die-cut aluminum sheet
    15.2 x 62.2 cm
39. View of three *Signs* in Dyck's studio
    beeswax on die-cut aluminum sheet
    (1) *Scientist*: 15.2 x 62.2 cm
    (2) *Larvae*: 15.2 x 43.2 cm
    (3) *Nurse*: 15.2 x 43.2 cm
40. Honeybees working on first line of the Braille poem
    for *Working in the Dark*, 1999
    photograph by William Eakin
41. *Poem to the Bees by Di Brandt* [one line of the poem], 2007-2008
    plywood, ink and beeswax on Braille paper
    dimensions variable
42. *Poem to the Bees by Di Brandt* [one line of the poem], 2007-2008
    plywood, ink and beeswax on Braille paper
    dimensions variable
43. *Poem to the Bees by Di Brandt*, 2007-2008
    installation view at Burnaby Art Gallery
    plywood, ink and beeswax on Braille paper
    dimensions variable
44. *Hive Scan*, 2001-2003
    collaboration between Aganetha and Richard Dyck
    cibachrome print on paper
    60.9 x 76.2 cm
45. *Hive Scan*, 2001-2003
    collaboration between Aganetha and Richard Dyck
    cibachrome print on paper
    60.9 x 76.2 cm
46. *Hive Scan*, 2001-2003
    collaboration between Aganetha and Richard Dyck

cibachrome print on paper
60.9 x 76.2 cm

47. *Hive Scan*, 2001-2003
collaboration between Aganetha and Richard Dyck
cibachrome print on paper
60.9 x 76.2 cm

48. *Hive Scan*, 2001-2003
collaboration between Aganetha and Richard Dyck
cibachrome print on paper
60.9 x 76.2 cm

49. *Hive Scan*, 2001-2003
collaboration between Aganetha and Richard Dyck
cibachrome print on paper
60.9 x 76.2 cm

50. *Hive Scan*, 2001-2003
collaboration between Aganetha and Richard Dyck
cibachrome print on paper
60.9 x 76.2 cm

51. *Hive Scan*, 2001-2003
collaboration between Aganetha and Richard Dyck
cibachrome print on paper
60.9 x 76.2 cm

52. *Aganetha Dyck and her Swarm of Bees* [detail], 2016-17
installation view at Tyler School of Art, Temple University
live honeybees, beeswax, and found objects in wooden cabinet

53. *Denouement: Memories of the Hive*, 2015
installation view at Tom Thomson Art Gallery
honeycomb on Feeder Boards
dimensions variable
exhibition curated by Virginia Eichhorn
photograph by Willy Waterton

54. *Feeder Boards*, 2016
installation view at Michael Gibson Gallery
honeycomb, drawings on Feeder Boards
dimensions variable
image courtesy Michael Gibson Gallery

55. *Beekeeper's Red Note*, 2012-16
    bee work and drawing on Feeder Board
    50.8 x 42.5 cm (20 x 16 3/4 inches)
    image courtesy Michael Gibson Gallery
56. *Honeybee's Alphabet*, 2012-16
    honeycomb, bee work on Feeder Board
    50.8 x 41.9 cm (20 x 16 1/2 inches)
    image courtesy Michael Gibson Gallery
57. *The Escape*, 2012-16
    metal, bee work and drawing on Feeder Board
    50.8 x 41.9 cm (20 x 16 1/2 inches)
    image courtesy Michael Gibson Gallery
58. *Secret Map of the Drawing Class*, 2012-16
    bee work and drawing on Feeder Board
    50.2 x 42.5 cm (19 3/4 x 16 3/4 inches)
    image courtesy Michael Gibson Gallery
59. *A Message From The Blind Beekeeper*, 2012-16
    bee work and drawing on Feeder Board
    50.8 x 42.5 cm (20 x 16 3/4 inches)
    image courtesy Michael Gibson Gallery
60. *Light*, 2011
    collaboration between Aganetha Dyck and William Eakin
    installation view at Michael Gibson Gallery
    image courtesy Michael Gibson Gallery
61. *Light*, 2011
    collaboration between Aganetha Dyck and William Eakin
    installation view at Michael Gibson Gallery
    image courtesy Michael Gibson Gallery
62. *Leaning Tower of Pisa*, 2011
    Aganetha Dyck
    found lamp, beeswax and honeycomb
    38.1 x 15.2 x 15.2 cm (15 x 6 x 6 inches)
    image courtesy Michael Gibson Gallery
63. *Light 0009*, 2011
    William Eakin
    photograph

33 x 48.2 cm (13 x 19 inches)
image courtesy William Eakin
64. *Light 0007*, 2011
William Eakin
photograph
33 x 48.2 cm (13 x 19 inches)
image courtesy William Eakin
65. *Pink Pillar with Couple*, 2011
Aganetha Dyck
found lamp, beeswax and honeycomb
33 x 20.3 x 12.7 cm (13 x 8 x 5 inches)
image courtesy Michael Gibson Gallery
66. *Light 0073*, 2011
William Eakin
photograph
33 x 48.2 cm (13 x 19 inches)
image courtesy William Eakin
67. *Green Hand*, 2011
Aganetha Dyck
found lamp, beeswax and honeycomb
46.9 x 15.2 x 15.2 cm (18 1/2 x 6 x 6 inches)
image courtesy Michael Gibson Gallery
68. Dyck removing *Lost Sculpture* from beehive, 1995
St. Norbert Arts and Cultural Centre Apiary
photograph by William Eakin
69. Aganetha and Michael Regan with *Park Bench* [in process], 1997
in Dyck's Yorkshire Sculpture Park studio
wooden bench, beeswax and mixed media
dimensions variable
70. Honeybees working on *Park Bench*, 1997
installed in Camellia House
wooden bench, beeswax and mixed media
dimensions variable
photographs by Peter Dyck
71. View of bee research in Dyck's studio, 2010
photograph by Miriam Jordan-Haladyn

72. Photograph of Aganetha and Peter Dyck at the beehives
73. Aganetha and Richard Dyck working on *Hive Scans*, 2001-2003
    photographs by Peter Dyck
74. Aganetha and Richard Dyck working on *Hive Scans*, 2001-2003
    photographs by Peter Dyck
75. *Altered Cigarettes and Cigars*, 1988
    installation view in Dyck's studio
    cigarettes, cigars and mixed media in Plexiglas display case
    dimensions variable
    photograph by Miriam Jordan-Haladyn
76. View of Dyck's drawings on the wall in her studio, 2010
    beeswax, pen and ink drawings on paper
    photograph by Miriam Jordan-Haladyn
77. View of Dyck's drawing on the wall in her studio, 2010
    ink on paper and wall
    photograph by Miriam Jordan-Haladyn
78. *Shrunken Sculpture*, 1976
    felt
    dimensions variable
    photographs by Peter Dyck
79. *Sizes 8 – 46*, 1978
    installation view in Plug In Gallery
    shrunken woolen clothes
    dimensions variable
80. *Canned Buttons*, 1984
    glass jars, buttons and wax
    dimensions variable
    photograph by Sheila Spence
81. *Canned Buttons*, 1984
    glass jars, buttons and wax
    dimensions variable
    photograph by Sheila Spence
82. *Shrunken Dress in Suitcase*, 1978-81
    shrunken woolen dress, gloves, found suitcase
    dimensions variable
    photograph by William Eakin

83. *Cabbages*, 1978 [in foreground]
    view of Dyck's 376 Donald studio
    found material
    dimensions variable
    photograph by William Eakin
84. Dyck and bees with *Sports Night in Canada* [football helmet], 1995
    installation view at St. Norbert Arts and Cultural Centre Apiary
    live honeybees, sports equipment and beeswax on beehive boxes
    dimensions variable
    image courtesy of Aganetha Dyck
85. Phil Veldhuis inspecting beehive, 1995
    St. Norbert Arts and Cultural Centre Apiary
    image courtesy of Aganetha Dyck
86. *Shrinks (Brown)*, 2012
    felted crochet, 100% wool
    60.9 x 43.1 x 30.4 cm (24 x 17 x 12 inches)
    image courtesy Michael Gibson Gallery
87. *Shrinks (Gold)*, 2012
    felted crochet, 100% wool
    45.7 x 33 x 30.4 cm (18 x 13 x 12 inches)
    image courtesy Michael Gibson Gallery
88. *Shrinks (Purple)*, 2012
    felted crochet, 100% wool
    41.9 x 40.6 x 33 cm (16 1/2 x 16 x 13 inches)
    image courtesy Michael Gibson Gallery
89. *Shrinks (Red)*, 2012
    felted crochet, 100% wool
    55.8 x 17.7 x 11.4 cm (22 x 7 x 4 1/2 inches)
    image courtesy Michael Gibson Gallery
90. *Denouement: Memories of the Hive*, 2015
    installation view at Tom Thomson Art Gallery
    exhibition curated by Virginia Eichhorn
    photograph by Willy Waterton
91. *Ancient Circle Print*, 2012-16
    paint and honeycomb on Feeder Board
    50.8 x 42.5 cm (20 x 16 3/4 inches)

image courtesy Michael Gibson Gallery
92. *The Apiary's Poem*, 2012-16
    honeycomb and bee work on Feeder Board
    50.8 x 41.9 cm (20 x 16 1/2 inches)
    image courtesy Michael Gibson Gallery
93. *Honeybees' Signature*, 2013
    honeycomb and bee work on hive frame fragment
    photograph by Julian Jason Haladyn

Bibliography

Sarah Alford, "A Collaboration with the Bees: The Art of Aganetha Dyck," *Hive Lights: The Canadian Honey Council* 16.3 (August 2003): 14, 16.

Barbra Amesbury, *Survivors In Search of a Voice* (Toronto: Woodlawn Arts Foundation, 1995), 36.

Karen Antaki, *Ordinary Magic: Aspects of Ritual in Contemporary Art* (Montréal: Leonard & Bina Ellen Art Gallery, 1995), 2, 10-11, 18-19, 20, 24.

Garry Apgar, Shaun Higgins and Colleen Striegel, *The Newspaper in Art* (Spokane: New Media Ventures, 1996), 167.

Renée Baert, *Trames De Mémoire/Materializing Memory* (Saint-Hyacinthe: Expression, centre d'exposition de Saint-Hyacinthe, 1996), 18-21.

Roger Balboni, Sylvie Marandon and Estelle Pagès, *Aganetha Dyck* (Paris: Services culturels de l'Ambassade du Canada, 2001).

Border Crossings Magazine, "Felt Feelings: Aganetha Dyck," *Border Crossings* 23.3 [issue 127] (August 2013): 17, 77-79.

Joan Borsa, "Performing Interconnectedness: The Cathartic Installations of Aganetha Dyck, Ann Hamilton and Susan Shantz," *n. paradoxa* 3 (1999): 24-29.

Joan Borsa, "The Absent Bride: Intimate Acts and Interior Movements," *Aganetha Dyck* (Winnipeg: Winnipeg Art Gallery and St. Norbert Arts & Cultural Centre, 1995): 50-58.

Joan Borsa, "We Have History, They Have Myth," *The Library: Inner/Outer* (Lethbridge: Art Gallery of Southern Alberta, 1991), 5-17.

Joan Borsa, *Another Prairies* (Toronto: The Art Gallery at Harbourfront, 1986), 4-5, 8-9.

Di Brandt and Aganetha Dyck, "Working in the Dark," *Ecclectica* (Arts Edition 2009): http://ecclectica.brandonu.ca/issues/2009/1/.

Di Brandt, *So This Is the World & Here I Am in It* (Edmonton: NeWest Press, 2007).

Brian Brennan, "Homage – Aganetha Dyck," *Galleries West* (Summer 2008): http://www.gallerieswest.ca/artists/previews/aganetha-dyck---homage/.

Sheila Butler, "Women's Work: The Radical Domestications of Aganetha Dyck," *Arts Manitoba* 4.1 (Winter 1984): 15-19.

Sigrid Dahle, "Talking with Aganetha Dyck: A Ten Year Conversation," *Aganetha Dyck* (Winnipeg: Winnipeg Art Gallery and St. Norbert Arts & Cultural Centre, 1995): 16-27.

Sigrid Dahle, *Hand Held: Between Index and Middle Fingers* (Vancouver: The Lateral Gallery, 1990).

Sigrid Dahle, *A Multiplicity of Voices: Work by Manitoba Women Artists* (Winnipeg: Gallery One One One, 1987), 5, 12-13.

Kate Davis, "Public Service and Strategic Marketing as Audience Development," *Canadian Museums Association: Muse* XIV.1 (Spring 1996).

Tess Edmonson, "Aganetha Dyck: A Hive of Activity," *Canadian Art* (August 2011): http://canadianart.ca/features/aganetha_dyck/.

Hattie Ellis, *Sweetness and Light: The Mysterious History of the Honeybee* (New York: Three Rivers Press, 2004).

Robert Enright, "The Incredible Lightness of Bee-ing" [introduction by Meeka Walsh], *Border Crossings* 19.2 (May 2000): 42-57.

Robert Enright, "Corpus" [review], *Canadian Art* 10.3 (Fall 1993): 80-81.

Cliff Eyland, "Aganetha Dyck," *C Magazine* (April/June 1996): 43

Gary Essar, *Aganetha Dyck: Recent Work* [brochure] (Winnipeg: The Winnipeg Art Gallery, 1984), np.

Emily Falvey, *Animal Intent* [brochure] (New York: apexart, 2016), np.

Len Findlay, "Rumours of Our Breath," *Border Crossings* 12.3 (July 1993): 50-53.

Ron Frohwerk and Gerry Kisil, *Off The Beaten Track: New Canadian Art* (Winnipeg: Ace Art, 1989), 7-8, 11-12,16, 26.

Alison Gillmor, "Objects of Wonder," *Border Crossings* 14.3 (Summer 1995): 22-23.

Bruce Grenville, "Chance, Abstraction, Expression: Aganetha Dyck's Shrunken Clothing," *Aganetha Dyck* (Winnipeg: Winnipeg Art Gallery and St. Norbert Arts & Cultural Centre, 1995): 28-31.

Bruce Grenville and Jessica Bradley, *Corpus* (Saskatoon: The Mendel Art Gallery, 1995), 12, 24-25.

Paula Gustafson, "Aganetha Dyck: The Fabric of Daily Existence," *Espace* 36 (1996): 34-36.

Terrence Heath, "Another Prairies" [review], *Border Crossings* 6.1 (Winter 1986): 28.

Gilles Hébert, "Aganetha Dyck and the St. Norbert Arts & Cultural Centre," *Aganetha Dyck* (Winnipeg: Winnipeg Art Gallery and St. Norbert Arts & Cultural Centre, 1995), 60-63.

Jan Jagodzinski, "An Avant-garde 'without Authority': Towards a Future Oekoumene—if there is a Future," *States of Crisis and Post-Capitalist Scenarios*, eds. Heiko Feldner, Fabio Vighi and Slavoj Zizek (London: Routledge, 2016), 219-240.

Anne Kerner, "Aganetha Dyck Tricot d'Abeilles," *Beaux Art* 202 (March 2001): 34.

Peter Kevan, "Beekeeping in Art II: Aganetha Dyck," *Hive Lights: The Canadian Honey Council* 29.2 (May 2016): 13-15.

Serena Keshavjee, "Aganetha Dyck: Nature as Language," *Aganetha Dyck: Nature as Language*, ed. Serena Keshavjee (Winnipeg: Gallery One One One, 2000): https://www.umanitoba.ca/schools/art/content/galleryoneoneone/dyck.html.

Sandra Kwock-Silve, "Art: Aganetha Dyck," *Paris Voice* (Paris, 2001).

Robin Laurence, "Aganetha Dyck: The Wild Lies All Around Us," *Aganetha Dyck: Collaborations* (Burnaby: Burnaby Art Gallery, 2009), 9-15.

Virginia MacDonnell, *Inter Species Communication Attempt* [brochure] (Toronto: DeLeon White Gallery, 2001), np.

Shirley Madill and Ivan Jurakic, *Zone 6B, art in the environment* (Hamilton: Hamilton Artists Inc., 2000).

Shirley Madill, "Out of the Home and into the Hive," *Aganetha Dyck* (Winnipeg: Winnipeg Art Gallery and St. Norbert Arts & Cultural Centre, 1995): 8-14.

Shirley Madill, "Aganetha Dyck and 200,000 Bees," *Tableau* 8.3 (May/June 1995): 2.

Shirley Madill, *Contemporary art in Manitoba* (Winnipeg: Winnipeg Art Gallery, 1987), 32, 91.

Shirley Madill, *Under Construction: Six Manitoba Sculptors* (Winnipeg: Winnipeg Art Gallery, 1982), 6, 12-15, 37.

Mason Journal, "Interview with Aganetha Dyck: Canadian Visual Artist," *Mason Journal* (2011): http://www.mason-studio.com/journal.

Elizabeth Martin and Vivian Meyer, *Female Gazes: Seventy-Five Women Artists* (Toronto: Second Story Press, 1997), 124.

Donna McAlear, *Cradles* [brochure] (Kamloops: Kamloops Art Gallery, 1985), np.

Anne McPherson, *Second Skin: Looking at the Garden Again* (Guelph: MacDonald Stewart Art Centre, 1996), 12.

Meghan McKnight, "Aganetha Dyck's Interspecies Communication Attempt at DeLeon White Gallery" [review], *Contrapposto* 1 (2002): 30-31.

Doug Melnyk, "Still Life: Aganetha Dyck & Karen Thorton," *Critical Distance* 1.13 (March/April 1995).

Shannon Moore, "A Poignant Farewell: Aganetha Dyck at the Tom Thomson Gallery," *National Gallery of Canada Magazine* (September 2015): http://www.ngcmagazine.ca/correspondents/a-poignant-farewell-aganetha-dyck-at-the-tom-thomson-gallery.

Andrea Philp, "A Peek into the Hive," *Tableau* 8.3 (May/June 1995): 3.

Carol Phillips, *Changes* [brochure] (Regina: Norman MacKenzie Art Gallery, 1978), np.

Juan Antonio Ramirez, *The Beehive Metaphor: From Gaudi to Le Corbusier* (London: Reaktion Books, 2000).

Juan Antonio Ramírez, "Aganetha Dyck: The Living Skin," *Aganetha Dyck: Nature as Language*, ed. Serena Keshavjee (Winnipeg:

Gallery One One One, 2000): https://www.umanitoba.ca/schools/art/content/galleryoneoneone/dyck.html.

Verna Reid, *Women Between: Construction of Self in the Work of Sharon Butala, Aganetha Dyck, Mary Meigs and Mary Pratt* (Calgary: University of Calgary Press, 2008).

Priscilla Reimer, *Mennonite Artist: Insider as Outsider* (Winnipeg: Main/Access Gallery, 1990), 13-14, 36-37.

Randy Jayne Rosenberg, *Nature's Toolbox: Biodiversity, Art, and Invention* (San Francisco: Natural World Museum, 2012), np.

Al Rushton, "Aganetha Dyck's Mad Hatting," *Border Crossings* 6.3 (June 1987): 25-26.

Linda Sawchyn and Jeremy Lanaway, *Break Away!* (Kelowna: Kelowna Art Gallery, 2004).

Grace E. Thomson, "The 'Art Cigarette' Resolution," *Brain is not Enough* (Winnipeg: Gallery One One One, 1988), 2-3.

Nancy Tousley, "Aganetha Dyck," *Canadian Art* 9.3 (Fall 1992): 60-65.

Sandra Vida and Sylvia Ziemann, *Mentoring: Manitoba Artists for Women's Art: A Catalytic Situation* (Calgary: The New Gallery, 1992), 11.

Meeka Walsh (ed.), *The Winnipeg Alphabestiary* (Winnipeg: Border Crossings Book, 2008).

Meeka Walsh, "Bee Work: Aganetha's Dyck Project-in-Progress," *Border Crossings* 10.4 (November 1991): 39-40.

Mark L. Winston, *Bee Time: Lessons from the Hive* (Cambridge: Harvard University Press, 2014).

Mark L. Winston, "Aganetha Dyck: Introduction: Science, Art, and Bees," *Aganetha Dyck: Nature as Language*, ed. Serena Keshavjee (Winnipeg: Gallery One One One, 2000): https://www.umanitoba.ca/schools/art/content/galleryoneoneone/dyck.html.

Marian Yeo, "Aganetha Dyck," *Woman's Art Journal* 8.1 (Spring/Summer 1987): 35-38.

Other titles in the CAMS series:

Madeline Lennon, *Shelley Niro: Seeing Through Memory*, 2014

www.ingramcontent.com/pod-product-compliance
Lightning Source LLC
Chambersburg PA
CBHW020644220526
45464CB00001B/293